TEACHING SOFT SKILLS IN A HARD WORLD

TEACHING SOFT SKILLS IN A HARD WORLD

Skills for Beginning Teachers

Nancy Armstrong Melser

ROWMAN & LITTLEFIELD
Lanham • Boulder • New York • London

Published by Rowman & Littlefield
An imprint of The Rowman & Littlefield Publishing Group, Inc.
4501 Forbes Boulevard, Suite 200, Lanham, Maryland 20706
www.rowman.com

6 Tinworth Street, London SE11 5AL

Copyright © 2019 by Nancy Armstrong Melser

All rights reserved. No part of this book may be reproduced in any form or by any electronic or mechanical means, including information storage and retrieval systems, without written permission from the publisher, except by a reviewer who may quote passages in a review.

British Library Cataloguing in Publication Information Available

Library of Congress Cataloging-in-Publication Data

Name: Melser, Nancy Armstrong
Title: Teaching soft skills in a hard world : Skills for beginning teachers
ISBN: 978-1-4758-4654-6 (cloth)
ISBN: 978-1-4758-4655-3 (paper)
ISBN: 978-1-4758-4656-0 (electronic)

CONTENTS

Preface	vii
Acknowledgments	ix
Introduction	1
1 Communication Skills	7
2 Confidence	15
3 Enthusiasm	23
4 Creativity	31
5 Decision-Making Skills	37
6 Teamwork and Collaboration	45
7 Stress Management	53
8 Positive Attitude	61
9 Adaptability and Flexibility	67
10 Time Management	75
11 Organization	83
12 Initiative	91
13 Professionalism	97
14 Work Ethic	105
Conclusion	111
Bibliography	117
About the Author	119

PREFACE

As a teacher educator for more than twenty-five years, I have worked with students in field experiences and practicums for quite some time. I have also supervised over three hundred student teachers in a variety of educational settings. Although the majority of my students have done well and left student teaching ready for the real world, a handful were lacking in the skills necessary for their future classrooms or were dismissed from their experience before reaching licensure.

I have always wondered how I could have helped these students to better understand the skills needed for teaching as well as assist mentor teachers and administrators with whom they were working. Often, when discussing competencies that were lacking, administrators would note that they weren't items on a rubric or ideas that were easy to measure; instead, they would say things like "I just can't put my finger on it," or "It's not a requirement on the list!" I have dealt with this issue for years, never quite sure how to fix it.

I decided to conduct a survey with school superintendents and other administrators, asking "What are our current student teachers lacking?" I wanted to identify the elements that were missing in student teachers or in need of remediation. One administrator's reply caught my eye: the simple phrase "soft skills." Not knowing anything about this term, I started researching it and realized it was exactly what I had been looking for.

Soft skills, according to Oxford Dictionary, are "personal attributes that enable someone to interact effectively and harmoniously with other people" (Oxford Dictionary 2018). They are the attributes, dispositions, and characteristics that teacher educators and school administrators have difficulty putting into words—the part of teacher-preparation programs constantly being revised in search of a clearer definition. These skills are the hardest to teach to pre-service teachers yet the most important component of getting a teaching job!

The term *soft skills* was first introduced in 1972 in an army training manual that focused on the competencies needed for leadership and training, especially effective communication and working well with others (US Army 1972). Today, the term is used in the business world to describe the characteristics needed to get hired and to retain a position. The skills are hard to quantify, and lists vary, depending on the source. However, no other books exist on the use of soft skills in the field of education.

This book is an attempt to identify the soft skills needed for the teaching profession as well as how to teach them to both pre-service and beginning teachers. While it's impossible to create an exhaustive list of the characteristics and dispositions needed for classroom teachers, this book contains what I feel are the most important soft skills necessary for a teaching career. I've based it on my experience in classrooms, observing both well-prepared students and those who were lacking in these beneficial abilities. In these pages I examine fourteen specific soft skills, as well as provide strategies for teacher educators and school personnel to use, to help guide pre-service and beginning teachers toward acquiring them for their future classrooms.

Soft skills are important for teachers to learn and model, and will also help universities, school administrators, and anyone involved in the teaching profession to assist those entering the field of education. The fourteen soft skills described in this book are not the only ones that could help beginning teachers in the classroom, but they do provide a good place to start. I hope that readers will gain valuable strategies to help pre-service and beginning teachers learn the soft skills that will help with communication and productivity, while still practicing the hard skills needed in today's classrooms. The students they will eventually educate deserve a teacher who is not only well prepared with pedagogy but also armed with the soft skills needed in today's challenging world.

ACKNOWLEDGMENTS

First, I would like to thank the many teachers and student teachers with whom I have worked over the years, including my friends and colleagues at Burris Laboratory School, Forest Dale Elementary, and Orchard Park Elementary.

Pat Clark, the chair of the Elementary Education Department at Ball State, was always helpful and encouraged me as I worked with beginning teachers.

Jon Dee and Sari Harris assisted in providing me with placements for my student teachers and helped with administering my initial surveys to administrators.

Thanks, also, to my colleagues at Ball State for being kind and caring throughout my teaching endeavors.

I would also like to thank my teacher friends, Jeanni Doyle and Nancy Wilson, for their encouragement and for learning with me when I, too, was a beginning teacher.

A special thanks to my friend and colleague, Ann Leitze, for being supportive and sharing teacher stories over Mexican food, and to my friend, Melinda Roberts, for doing the same over a glass of wine.

To my cousin, Sue Brumbaugh—thanks for being both a friend and mentor. You were always a teacher I looked up to in life.

I want to thank my parents, Bill and Joan Armstrong, for their love and support over the years. My mom, a teacher for thirty-four years, helped me with the teaching skills in this book, and my dad taught me about the professional aspects, such as having a good work ethic.

Thank you to my editor, Tom Koerner. I appreciated his guidance and encouragement while writing my first book.

Finally, to all of the teachers who have yet to enter the field of education—remember that teaching is a noble profession, and practicing these soft skills will help you with the most precious job the world has to offer—educating our children.

INTRODUCTION

- **Soft skills versus hard skills**
- **Impact of soft skills on teacher-education students and beginning teachers**
- **Explanation of soft skills and ideas for using this book**

Soft skills, according to the Oxford Dictionary, are "personal attributes that enable someone to interact effectively and harmoniously with other people" (Oxford Dictionary 2018). Soft skills include the characteristics, attributes, and competencies needed to teach children as well as interact with colleagues and parents. They are the interpersonal skills that help beginning teachers relate to their students and teach the concepts needed in classrooms. The list is limitless and may vary from person to person, or even day to day.

Soft skills are the attributes that people have which enable them to communicate, work together, and get along with others. They are also key components of securing and keeping a job, such as being organized and having a good work ethic. Soft skills are hard to measure yet necessary in today's classrooms. Educators who have worked with teacher education students or beginning teachers know exactly what soft skills are needed to be a successful teacher.

University supervisors, mentor teachers, and school faculty members often have a hard time pinpointing exactly what is lacking in a preservice teacher's performance. Comments like "It's hard to measure on a rubric" and "There are just no words to explain her behaviors" often clue them in that the missing element is a soft skill. Although these skills may be hard to evaluate, it's obvious they are definitely lacking in some inexperienced teachers. They clearly delineate the difference between a proficient and a distinguished future educator, as outstanding educators exhibit the soft skills described in this book.

SOFT SKILLS VERSUS HARD SKILLS

Soft skills are the characteristics and dispositions that are exhibited in the classroom. They include items like strong communication and decision-making skills, along with other attributes that make teachers successful in their classrooms. In contrast to hard skills, they are often difficult to measure and explain in a simple list.

On the other hand, hard skills in the field of education are easy to teach. They are typically listed as objectives on course syllabi and measured on teacher-evaluation instruments. Hard skills in teaching include elements like lesson planning, creating classroom assessments, and discipline and classroom management. A student in a teacher-education program can learn the basic elements of a lesson plan and produce a quality blueprint that contains all of the necessary pieces for a successful lesson. Pre-service teachers can also learn how to create assessments and tests to evaluate the learning of children and decide whether or not they have mastered a particular concept. They can be rated on a rubric to decide if the proper testing techniques were used and if the evaluation was fair and accurate. It is easy to determine whether this hard skill (the assessment) was in place and accurate.

A pre-service teacher can be observed and evaluated for proper classroom management skills and a positive classroom environment. Items such as effective transitions and genuine praise and feedback can be videotaped to watch and self-evaluate to determine the great things in the lesson versus the items to keep working on. These hard skills are teachable, and it's easy to determine if the skills are in place or not.

The difference between soft and hard skills is that hard skills can be easily taught, modeled, and evaluated. They can be measured on a rubric or seen in an observation. Hard skills are the items listed as objectives on college syllabi or teaching-evaluation instruments, and straightforward methods are used to measure whether they have been successfully demonstrated. Soft skills, on the other hand, are the dispositions and attributes that make a new teacher unique—and ultimately successful—in the teaching profession.

Soft skills are the important characteristics found in pre-service or beginning teachers that allow them to communicate, get along, and participate in the professional community of teaching. They also allow new teachers to make decisions, be flexible, and learn from new situations. Soft skills include the value of a good work ethic and the ability to use appropriate stress-management skills in tough situations. Though they may not be easy to measure, they are important to the success of pre-service teachers and the quality of teaching they will eventually provide to students in their classrooms.

Soft skills are also related to the term *dispositions* in the teaching profession. Professional organizations such as the Council for the Accreditation of Teacher Preparation (CAEP) define dispositions as "The habits of professional action and moral commitments that underlie an educator's performance" (CAEP 2018). Dispositions are taught and assessed in teacher-education programs for pre-service teachers as well as on teaching-evaluation instruments for both beginning and veteran teachers. They evaluate the professionalism and teaching actions that educators make on a daily basis.

In 2016, the American Association of Colleges for Teacher Preparation (AACTE) created standards for High-Quality Teacher Preparation. Among these standards is the "importance of accreditation, particularly its role in assuring that the preparation of professional educators ultimately serves the interests and learning of PK–12 students" (AACTE 2016). Soft skills are directly related to this standard, as they impact the professional preparation of teachers.

In addition, the Association of Teacher Educators (ATE) has Standards for Teacher Educators. Standard One states that "In order for teacher educators to impact the profession, they must successfully model appropriate behaviors in order for those behaviors to be observed, adjusted, replicated, internalized, and applied appropriately to learners of all levels and styles" (ATE 2018).

By exhibiting appropriate teacher behaviors and being professional in the classroom, teachers are modeling the competencies that will help students ultimately value these skills as well. The dispositions and characteristics of outstanding teachers are easy to see, and the soft skills that are lacking in poor teachers are simple to assess.

Soft skills and teacher dispositions are almost synonymous in that they both describe the personal actions and skills teachers need in order to succeed, even though they may be difficult to observe and evaluate. Teacher educators and administrators know that all teachers need soft skills in order to be productive and teach children, yet they are not found on a concrete list or evaluation instrument. They are often fluid, changing with the needs of the children in one's classroom, and they can vary, depending on an educator's background and experiences.

The following will explain why the fourteen soft skills included in this book are important to beginning educators.

IMPACT OF SOFT SKILLS ON TEACHER-EDUCATION STUDENTS AND BEGINNING TEACHERS

Each school year, teachers enter classrooms full of children who are eager to learn and interested in discovering new information. These teachers need to have basic teaching skills, such as classroom management and lesson planning, yet also require the soft skills needed to teach and communicate with the children in their classrooms.

Teachers who are equipped with effective communication skills, a good work ethic, and a positive attitude are far more likely to make learning fun and relative to a child's life. They can communicate information more effectively and solve problems more quickly, and they possess organization and time management skills that help classrooms run more smoothly. These teachers also serve as role models for their students, who will need these soft skills in their own future careers.

Though soft skills are sometimes addressed through disposition rubrics in teacher-education programs, they are often not built in as required lessons in most university classrooms. They are the skills learned during teaching episodes and when working with children. Sometimes, soft skills are even learned through natural consequences, such as learning a lesson about preparedness when one wakes up late and is not prepared and ready for school. These soft skills are needed on a daily basis in both elementary and secondary classrooms. Teachers need to practice effective communication skills, have proper organization in their classrooms, and be able to work collaboratively with others in the school building. Not only do they need these skills to do their jobs, but they are also modeling them for student teachers and children in their classrooms.

Knowing that children are *always* watching is another reason that soft skills are important in the classroom. As teachers model behaviors, both good and bad, children are observing how to work with others, how to use appropriate manners, and when to use certain deeds and actions. This modeling by teachers has a direct impact on children and their eventual behavior in classrooms. Teachers have an important role in the education of children, and the results are not always demonstrated by the facts their students can recite or the test scores they receive.

This book will introduce fourteen of the most important soft skills in the field of education. It will explain how each skill is used in teaching as well as ideas for how to model and explain them in college classrooms, field experiences, and student teaching. The chapters also contain ideas for administrators and mentor teachers who are working with beginning teachers. By learning to implement these fourteen skills, pre-service and beginning teachers will learn professional behaviors that will help them obtain—and keep—jobs. They will also learn to use appropriate teaching skills in the classroom and model suitable conduct in the classroom.

It is my hope that this book will ultimately help pre-service education students and beginning teachers to become successful instructors and models of good citizenship in their future classrooms, passing these invaluable lessons on to their own students.

I

COMMUNICATION SKILLS

- Why are communication skills important?
- How do I teach and model communication skills?
- What are some activities to practice communication skills?

IMPORTANCE OF COMMUNICATION SKILLS IN TEACHING

Communication skills are perhaps one of the most important soft skills in the teaching profession. Without the ability to communicate proficiently, teachers will have difficulty teaching concepts, relating to children, and working with colleagues and parents. It is through communication that teachers let students know they are doing well; they can also communicate through body language when students are not showing proper behavior.

Communication includes the correct usage of written and spoken language. This is important, as teachers model this characteristic to children on a daily basis, and students are quick to notice proper grammar and language in the classroom.

Instructional skills have been taught and modeled in teacher-preparation programs since the beginning of this career. The entire purpose of a teacher is to share new knowledge and information. However, not all teachers are distinguished communicators. Sometimes speaking in front of a group, meeting with colleagues, and conferencing with parents can be intimidating to new teachers. Although this skill may seem difficult to many, it is one that is only improved with experience.

Communication is the ability to use the skills of reading, writing, listening, and speaking. However, it can also include items like nonverbal communication, where someone can read *body language* to tell how another person is feeling, or if he/she is happy. All of these skills combined make the skill of communication a vital part of teaching.

Interacting with children is perhaps the most important soft skill in the profession of teaching, as the entire point of being an educator is communicating and teaching new concepts to one's students. Being able to teach new information on the level of children, and in a developmentally appropriate way, is a key to relating concepts in classrooms. Remembering to associate concepts to the students' backgrounds and knowledge is recommended. If a student does not have the proper schema and background information, it is very hard to comprehend what is being taught.

Another aspect of communicating with children is in giving directions. Beginning and new teachers need to be taught the importance of giving clear directions and modeling procedures and techniques for the students. They also need to know the importance of *telling* rather than *asking* students to do something. Beginning teachers often start lessons with phrases such as "Johnny, would you like to join us at the carpet?" or "Johnny, come to the reading center, okay?" which are clearly different from "Johnny, please come to the carpet now." Simply telling the directions as a statement implies that the child needs to follow the direction given, as opposed to asking, which is seen as a choice.

Communication skills with children also include body language and other nonverbal forms of communication. Beginning teachers frequently learn the use of *the teacher look*—the inevitable look that teachers have perfected that lets children know their current behavior is unacceptable. Often, just a glance at an inappropriate behavior or a finger to the lips can do more than words can convey. Perfecting this look with children and students can allow a teacher to have effective classroom management, without ever saying a word!

Working with families is also a vital soft skill for beginning teachers. It's important to learn how to effectively communicate both in person and digitally with the families in one's classroom. In the college classroom, participating in mock parent–teacher conferences can be a valuable tool. Participating in scenarios with diverse situations can also be very beneficial. Working through scenarios which involve an upset grandmother, LGBTQ families, or parents who have recently divorced can provide experience for handling these situations in the future.

Communicating with families and recognizing their value makes them feel welcome and important in the school setting. Teachers show children that school is a safe and inspiring place and that parents and schools work together to educate all children who enter. Knowing that many people care about their education is important for children to learn from a very early age. Perfecting the skill of communication with families is important to pre-service and beginning teachers who will ultimately interact with others to benefit the children in their classrooms.

Another part of communication which needs to be addressed in the digital age is that of electronic communication, including e-mail, class newsletters, and social media. As these modes of communication become more popular, it is important for pre-service and beginning teachers to be aware of appropriate uses for these tools. Valuable things to remember include using concise wording and proper grammar and avoiding acronyms and educational jargon. While social media is a powerful tool, providing immediate access for parents, it is very important to know the etiquette for such use, which includes being aware of personal accounts that parents and families can enter. Teaching pre-service and beginning teachers to watch the posting of inappropriate photos, personal information, and other documents that one would not normally share with families of the children one is teaching is vital to both confidentiality and the morality clauses which appear in many teaching contracts.

Communication via technology also includes the use of appropriate texting and e-mail strategies. It is important for teachers to model proper spelling and grammar for their students and the parents with whom they may be communicating, spelling out shortened texting acronyms (e.g., "I don't know" rather than IDK). Also important to remember is that the tone of an e-mail can be interpreted quite differently than a sender may have intended. Sometimes, picking up the phone or meeting in person can be much more effective than sending an e-mail.

The disposition of effective communication is a very important soft skill for both pre-service and beginning teachers. By learning to correspond with families and administrators, and teaching effectively with both verbal and nonverbal skills, new teachers will learn an important aspect of teaching that will be used in future classrooms. Also, remembering to use proper etiquette while on social media can be a valuable and meaningful part of communication skills for future teachers.

HOW TO MODEL THESE SKILLS FOR BEGINNING TEACHERS

In order to learn the soft skill of communication, one must first learn by proper modeling. Having professors and mentor teachers who model the appropriate use of grammar, spelling, and other communication strategies is highly important to pre-service teachers, who are always watching.

Also, modeling skills such as giving directions to children is important, as much of teaching involves explaining and providing directions. Learning how to give directions in a concise yet accurate way is often difficult for beginning teachers, as they sometimes give directions too quickly. At the other extreme, sometimes they provide information that is too detailed and not developmentally appropriate. By watching a mentor teacher model how this is done, both pre-service teachers and children in classrooms will benefit.

Another communication skill which is vital to teach and model for beginning teachers is communication with administrators. Learning how to approach an administrator in a professional and respectful way can lead to career recommendations and jobs in the future. Learning that one does not begin an e-mail to a school principal with "Hey" is important and timely in today's digital world. Perhaps a mentor teacher and student teacher could construct such e-mails together to learn this very important skill.

Communicating with colleagues is also an important part of this soft skill. As more schools are using a collaborative approach to teaching and provide team planning time for grade-level/subject-area teams, it's more important than ever to learn the skill of working with other teachers. Before entering one's first teaching position, it's helpful to learn how and when to voice one's opinion and to hone one's ability to work with a difficult colleague.

Since communication is the main source of teaching, it is important to understand how to teach and model good communication skills for new teachers. The following will provide examples of ways to do this.

ACTIVITIES TO PRACTICE THESE SKILLS WITH NEW TEACHERS

As stated previously, learning through proper modeling is probably the most important part of teaching this skill to beginning teachers. However, there are also many other ways that pre-service teachers and new teachers can learn this skill. The following are some other ideas to help teach communication skills in college classes and school settings.

In addition to seeing proper modeling, another important part of learning effective communication skills is simply being given the opportunity to practice them. Encouraging pre-service teachers to interact with children and students at a very early stage of their college career is very important. Offering field experiences and practicums often and early can provide beginning teachers with the opportunity to learn this skill in the real world. Allowing pre-service teachers the opportunity to interact in small group lessons, do read-alouds with children, or work in informal settings, such as afterschool programs, are all options. Having time with students is an important step toward learning communication in the teaching profession.

As colleges and universities focus more on providing early classroom experience for new teachers, it is also important to stress proper written and spoken grammar. Since teachers are modeling the use of proper language, appropriate subject–verb agreement, and avoidance of slang, they also need to practice and refine these skills in their college classes. Having rubrics which evaluate and grade written and spoken grammar are important guides to ensure that this happens in college courses.

An additional way to encourage communication skills in pre-service teachers and beginning teachers is through practice lessons and appropriate feedback. Even if the college can't arrange sufficient time to work with children in real classrooms, universities can create practice lessons with feedback from professors and classmates.

Communication strategies are a skill that can only be improved with practice. By doing mock lessons with peer feedback, pre-service teachers can discover if their lesson is making sense, if the information is correct, and whether it is interesting—even without children present!

Finally, beginning teachers and education majors can learn communication skills by practicing them in classrooms and during field experiences. Being allowed to write a parent letter (with supervision, of course) and practice their communication skills through real-life experiences can greatly benefit beginning teachers. Learning how to write report-card comments and providing feedback to both parents and children is another important teaching skill. Being able to participate in as many real-life teaching experiences as possible is a key to preparing future teachers for their classrooms.

Learning to communicate with technology is another important skill for beginning teachers. As technology is used more in today's classrooms, learning the effective use of tools such as document cameras, Smart Boards, and other hardware is essential to successful teaching. It can be tricky for beginning teachers to use the equipment while remaining aware of their students at the same time. Being able to load paper into the document camera while still scanning the room and watching for misbehaviors takes time and experience to learn and develop. Practicing this skill with children in field placements and student teaching provides new teachers with valuable experience they will be able to draw on in future classrooms.

Overall, the skill of effective communication is one of the most important soft skills that a beginning teacher can learn. Being able to teach effective lessons through direct instruction, small group interaction, and individual activities with children is an initial step in preparing teachers for the real world of their classrooms. In addition, learning to communicate with administrators, colleagues, and parents is another important skill for new teachers to learn before stepping foot in their own classrooms. If a pre-service or beginning teacher is not proficient in the skill of communication, they will find other areas of teaching to be very difficult indeed.

KEY IDEAS

- Communication skills are important for many reasons, especially in teaching and sharing new information with children.

- Communication includes proper grammar and appropriate modeling, important skills when working with students.
- Body language and facial expressions are also part of effective communication.
- Working with colleagues and administrators is an important aspect of good communication.
- Communication with parents and families is a vital skill in teaching and needs to be modeled and practiced.
- Technology, including social media, is significant in teaching, and teachers need to communicate professionally on these platforms at all times.

2

CONFIDENCE

- Why is confidence an important skill for beginning teachers?
- How can I model confidence in the classroom?
- What are some activities to promote confidence with a preservice or beginning teacher?

IMPORTANCE OF CONFIDENCE IN TEACHING

Confidence, or the idea of believing in oneself, is a valuable soft skill for new teachers. Being in front of a classroom of students can be an intimidating and fearful experience. It takes self-confidence and a certain amount of acting skill for a new teacher to succeed when they see their students, who expect them to know all the answers. The saying *Never let them see you sweat* is the ultimate description of having confidence in the classroom. Children, even as young as preschool, can tell when a teacher is unprepared, scared, or unsure of himself. They know if a teacher is self-assured and ready, or if she is feeling anxious or worried. They also know that a teacher who's not confident is easy to distract, move off task, or stress out, with little to no effort!

Being confident and *acting* like one knows what to do is half the battle. Even if things do not go exactly as planned, a disruption takes place, or a lesson goes off track, pretending to be in charge truly works. Portraying that one is in charge and in control shows that the teacher is confident and comfortable—even if one does not feel that way on the inside.

According to Alex Quigley, author of *The Confident Teacher* (2016), "Authentic confidence for a teacher stems from the trust we secure from our students and our colleagues. It becomes a trust we hold deeply within ourselves and helps guide what we do." By having the skill of confidence, teachers will be able to be more comfortable in the classroom and do their jobs in a meaningful and professional way.

Being confident also includes being prepared and looking like one is in control by not fidgeting, acting nervous, or appearing anxious. It also includes looking the part. The term *Dress for success* implies that the teacher dresses appropriately and wears clothing that is a bit more *adult* than what their students are wearing. Confidence also includes being able to think ahead, anticipate problems, and keep going—even if the lesson takes an unplanned turn.

The phrases *thinking on one's feet, winging it*, and *fake it till you make it* are all applicable to a teacher who displays confidence. Although every lesson should have a clear plan for teaching, sometimes the plan simply changes or takes a different turn. A confident teacher can make an unplanned event turn into a teachable moment and quickly revamp the plans to make them fit the situation.

A confident teacher also knows when to ask for help. Being confident does not mean that a teacher has to know all of the answers in a classroom. In fact, some of the most experienced veteran teachers find that asking for help and brainstorming possible solutions can be beneficial and even improves their confidence in the long run.

In all, confidence is a soft skill that comes with time and experience, through learning from prior mistakes, and from acting the part of the teacher, even when one is nervous on the inside. By modeling confidence, students will trust that their teacher is capable and will be less likely to challenge authority. Students who sense weakness and a lack of confidence in their teachers will take advantage of this uncertainty. If a teacher is prepared and ready, and believes in his or her abilities as a teacher, confidence will follow. It simply takes time to develop.

The next section will explain how instructors and mentor teachers can model the skill of confidence for pre-service and beginning teachers.

HOW TO MODEL THIS SKILL FOR BEGINNING TEACHERS

College instructors and mentor teachers can teach and model confidence in the classroom in various ways. One of the easiest strategies is simply by showing comfort and confidence in the classroom. Mentors who are self-assured (but not arrogant) come across as being in charge of the classroom, knowing the material they are about to teach, and confident in their abilities as an educator. They have students who show respect and trust that they have the knowledge and integrity to do the right thing and teach them in the best ways possible.

Mentor teachers and college instructors also model confidence in the area of teacher education by knowing how to educate new teachers with patience, kindness, and compassion. Remembering that they were once beginners, realizing that others helped induct them into the teaching profession, helps them do their job with humility and grace. Although college professors and mentor teachers sometimes need to have uncomfortable conversations with the pre-service students in their classrooms, this can be done in a constructive way, which includes pointing out both strengths and weaknesses. Developing goals and a professional growth plan will help beginning teachers learn how to improve certain behaviors and gain confidence, all with the help of a veteran classroom teacher.

Another way that mentor teachers can help teach the skill of confidence is by sharing their own stories with pre-service teachers. Everyone has a story about their first years of teaching—a mistake they once made or a classroom observation that did not go well. Sharing these stories with new teachers will help them to realize that everyone started somewhere, and mistakes are just part of the learning experience.

Pointing out times in the present where one's confidence might not be as solid can also help to model this skill for new teachers. Even veteran teachers with many of years of experience have moments when they don't feel as confident as they would like to be. A conference with an angry parent, a classroom observation by a school administrator, or a lesson in a brand-new curriculum are all times that veteran teachers may not feel as confident as they might like to feel. Sharing these conversations with new teachers, as well as a plan for dealing with these types of situations, can be helpful.

Allowing the pre-service or student teacher to assist in brainstorming this *plan of attack* can be advantageous. For example, if a teacher is getting ready for a conference with an upset parent, asking the pre-service teacher to help prepare some positive insights about the child, and writing down some examples of the work or behavior that is being discussed at the conference, can help model the fact that preparedness is one of the keys to entering uncomfortable situations.

Another way to help build confidence in beginning teachers is to encourage them to try new strategies and do things that might be just plain uncomfortable. When student teachers are encouraged and motivated to take risks and leave their comfort zones, they will learn that it is acceptable to venture into the unknown—even if the lesson or strategy is not perfect. Debriefing and brainstorming about the new strategy or the unfamiliar content that was taught will help new teachers realize that taking risks can be helpful and will allow the mentor teacher and student teacher to discuss what went well along with what did not. Through this discussion, pre-service teachers will realize that even though the new strategy might not have gone perfectly, trying new things is a useful and lifelong part of teaching.

Sharing and talking with beginning teachers about strategies for feeling confident, as well as the ways in which a mentor teacher deals with her own insecurities or uncertainties, can help new teachers realize that confidence takes time and experience to develop. By bringing up the issue of confidence, mentor teachers can address how this affects teaching, and work on ways to help make this soft skill stronger for the classroom.

The next section provides some ideas for activities to help beginning teachers develop the skill of confidence in the classroom.

ACTIVITIES TO PRACTICE THIS SKILL WITH NEW TEACHERS

Teaching is a profession that requires confidence: One has to manage a classroom, engage in public speaking, and be responsible for the learning of children, all in one job. It can be intimidating and stressful for beginning teachers, and learning confidence is an important way to prepare them for this adventure. By practicing this skill before obtaining a first teaching job, pre-service teachers can be more confident and comfortable in everything they do.

One of the first and most obvious ways to build confidence in new teachers is to put them in front of students as soon as possible. By offering early field experiences, where pre-service teachers interact and work with children, they will soon learn whether this is the profession they should enter. Simple tasks, such as working with a small group of students, doing a read-aloud with younger students, or preparing some icebreaker activities to get to know the students, are great ways to build basic confidence in working with children.

By starting gradually and introducing a practicum or student teacher to the class, the children will get to know the new adult in their classroom and will allow relationships to be built among them. In addition, reinforcing the idea of co-teaching and a shared classroom responsibility will help. Sharing the discipline plan and classroom rules with a student teacher and insisting that they follow the same routines will also be important in teaching them to be confident.

Telling the student teacher that the mentor teacher believes in him and supports him in management and teaching will also do a great deal to help teach confidence. If the mentor teacher and student teacher are *on the same page* philosophically, the students will see a united front and will be more likely to follow the rules and guidance of the teachers. At the same time, the student teacher will see himself more as a *real* teacher, thereby increasing his own confidence, as well.

Another way to practice confidence is by having a beginning teacher make a list or write a reflection of the skills they do well and the items they still need to work on in the teaching profession. Most beginning teachers can be very critical of themselves. Simply reflecting on the skills they already do have can help them to realize there are many positive aspects of their teaching. Sometimes, confidence is just about seeing the positive and not dwelling on the negative.

Videotaping and reflecting on one's teaching can also help to build confidence. Watching a video of one's lesson and monitoring for voice, self-control, and composure can help a beginning teacher see when confidence is present, or lacking, in a lesson. Self-reflection can help a beginning teacher troubleshoot and make plans to remediate areas of concern.

In addition to watching oneself teach on videos, observing veteran teachers is also a great idea. Pre-service teachers are often amazed by how confident veteran teachers are—how they can handle student behaviors with little effort, and how they communicate with children. Observing some self-assured teachers will provide beginning teachers with someone to model themselves after and will instill a sense of motivation in new teachers. Most building administrators can recommend a teacher or two to observe, and most confident teachers are more than happy to assist.

Another activity to help beginning teachers learn confidence is to notice when a beginning teacher is doing well and improving in the classroom. An interactive journal between the mentor teacher and student teacher can list such *noticings* and provide additional feedback about improvements and strengths. Some teachers use strategies such as *Three Stars and a Wish*, in which a mentor teacher lists three positive elements in a lesson and one item she wishes would still be improved. Making these quick notes and providing simple feedback on a prepared form is time-saving and beneficial. By providing some quick and positive feedback and noticing more good than bad in a lesson, a student teacher's confidence is bound to increase. Everyone likes to hear what he/she is doing well!

In brief, confidence is the idea of believing in oneself as a teacher. It is important that beginning teachers know what they do well, along with what they need to work on. Learning to improve and be confident and self-assured is vital, as children view the teacher the way the teacher sees himself. If a teacher is unsure and unprepared, the students will see the teacher in that same light. However, if they see a self-assured, confident teacher, they will be more likely to trust and respond.

KEY IDEAS

- Confidence is the idea of believing in one's teaching abilities and other attributes in the classroom.
- Confidence is a skill that takes years to develop and increases with experience.
- Even veteran teachers have moments when they do not feel confident. Sharing this with beginning teachers can be very helpful.

- Confidence is grown by having early teaching experiences and building relationships with students.
- Nurturing confidence with positive feedback and constructive criticism can help a beginning teacher grow.
- A teacher who has confidence will be more likely to be comfortable, poised, and self-assured. Students who see a confident teacher are more likely to follow directions and be respectful.

3

ENTHUSIASM

- Why is enthusiasm important to beginning teachers?
- How can I model this skill for pre-service and beginning teachers?
- What are some activities that can be used to practice this skill?

IMPORTANCE OF ENTHUSIASM IN TEACHING

Like confidence, the soft skill of enthusiasm is also noticed by students and teachers alike. Teachers who love their jobs enter the classroom with enthusiasm and a passion for the profession. They love what they are doing and continue to enjoy the job year after year. They make even the most monotonous lessons interesting and have classrooms that are inviting and fun. Teachers with enthusiasm motivate children to learn and help them discover new and exciting information. Enthusiasm is a dynamic that makes teachers memorable and children want to come to school. The energy and vigor that an enthusiastic teacher puts into lessons is what makes learning fun and enjoyable. According to the National Communication Association (NCA),

> An enthusiastic teacher often spices the class with excitement, enjoyment, and anticipation; engages students to participate; and stimulates them to explore. Thus, teacher enthusiasm sparks the curiosity of students and jumpstarts their motivation to learn. Teacher enthusiasm can lead to better teaching evaluations, positive attitudes to-

ward teachers, better student performance, and improved classroom behavior. (NCA 2014)

Teachers who exhibit enthusiasm make students feel welcomed, valued, and respected. A teacher who is enthusiastic about teaching creates students who will be enthusiastic about learning. An enthusiastic teacher invites students into the lesson and teaches in a way that keeps them there. From the passion to teach, to the extra energy in a lesson, teachers who are enthusiastic are the ones who are memorable and respected by their students.

Enthusiasm is said to be contagious. If a teacher arrives at school in a bad mood and teaches lessons in a mediocre way, the children are likely to respond in the same manner. However, if a teacher is excited and interested in the lesson, the children are far more likely to be engaged as well. In addition, enthusiasm is motivating to students. Teachers who are excited about the lesson they are teaching are more likely to create fun and engaging lessons and motivate children to learn as a result. By motivating students to learn, a teacher can create lifelong learners and teach the importance of exploring new ideas in the world around them.

Enthusiasm is also memorable. Teachers who are enthusiastic create lessons that are unforgettable and teach with strategies that reach all of the children in their classroom. If a teacher uses more exciting methods to teach, the students are likely to remember the information more clearly than lessons that are boring and uneventful.

So what if the content one is supposed to teach just isn't exciting? Make it so! Using creativity and enthusiasm in a lesson are worth the extra effort, and the students will be more engaged. Sometimes just spicing up a lesson with a fun activity or a different approach can make all the difference in the classroom tone and the learning that occurs.

In addition, students who are actively engaged by an enthusiastic teacher have far less time to misbehave. If a student is doing a hands-on lesson and is busy working, he/she will likely be on task and simply not have the time to act out. Busy students who focus on the lesson and are truly involved in activities show better behavior and learn more, simply because they are on task. An enthusiastic teacher makes sure this happens in the classroom.

Enthusiasm is not a cure for every problem in teaching. However, a teacher who comes to school excited and eager to teach will make learning new, will enjoy his/her job much more, and will feel involved and appreciated. Students who have enthusiastic teachers see role models who love learning and inquiry and are more likely to discover a love of learning as well.

The next section will focus on ways to model and teach this soft skill to pre-service teachers.

HOW TO MODEL THIS SKILL FOR BEGINNING TEACHERS

Imagine entering a classroom that appears drab and colorless, with a teacher who speaks in a monotone voice and hands out worksheets for every lesson. There is no energy, no love of learning, and no eagerness to discover. Then imagine entering a bright and cheerful classroom, with a teacher who smiles and displays enthusiasm and clearly loves learning. The teacher does hands-on activities, and the children are engaged and on task, simply because the teacher makes the lesson sound so exciting! Which place would you rather be?

The lack of enthusiasm in the first scenario is obvious, as it impacts both the teacher and the students in the classroom. However, the presence of enthusiasm in the second scenario represents energy, curiosity, and a teacher who motivates children to learn. The soft skill of enthusiasm is the key to success and creating students who enjoy learning.

Enthusiasm is a skill which is not always automatic in beginning teachers. Sometimes new teachers are shy, scared, or unsure of the material they are about to teach. Remembering to be enthusiastic and interested can be a soft skill that will help to alleviate these problems. Even if the topic of the lesson is not the most exciting, a good teacher can make anything sound fun! It is all about how the lesson is approached.

Obviously, modeling enthusiasm in one's teaching is one of the best ways to teach enthusiasm to beginning teachers. Pre-service teachers will observe and pick up on the efforts of a mentor teacher and realize that enthusiastic teachers can capture the attention of students and motivate them to learn.

Another technique for investigating enthusiasm is to videotape the student teacher teaching a lesson. Instead of focusing just on the teaching, however, focus on the students as well. Noting the engagement, involvement, and interaction of the children will provide a clear picture of the student teacher's enthusiasm. If students look bored, unengaged, and disruptive, a possible reason is that the lesson just wasn't interesting.

Being around other teachers who have a passion and enthusiasm for teaching is also a great way to model this skill for beginning teachers. Teachers who are negative and have no excitement for teaching can be detrimental to beginning teachers. Surrounding oneself with other teachers who exhibit the skill of enthusiasm is a great way to model this for pre-service and beginning teachers.

Watching motivational videos and placing encouraging posters in the classroom are also great ways to model enthusiasm for learning. If students see daily reminders of enthusiasm and positivity, they will be reminded that the teacher believes in them, that their efforts are worthwhile, and that they have a teacher who cares about their learning. Sometimes a visual reminder will help to encourage students and remind them to be enthusiastic about their own learning. Motivational videos about teaching are numerous on the Internet, and watching a video on the importance of passion in teaching can help motivate a beginning teacher to provide this skill in the classroom. Everyone has bad days, even in the teaching profession. Watching a quick video made by someone who is passionate about their teaching can remind beginning teachers why this profession is so important.

Keeping a *Good News Folder* is also a great way to model enthusiasm and energy in the classroom. Encouraging new teachers to keep the positive notes from administrators, a copy of a kind e-mail from a parent, or a sweet drawing from a student can be useful in the future.

On those days when a new teacher just doesn't have their normal enthusiasm for learning, or has a bad day in the classroom, they can reach into the Good News Folder to remind themselves of why they are teachers. Rereading the notes can renew their enthusiasm, and a mentor teacher can model the skill of reflection through the good news that they have saved.

Enthusiasm in the classroom is a key to both teacher and student success. Teachers who are passionate about their jobs and project a love of learning will create students who want to do the same. Also, enthusiasm and energy will make the days go by quickly, spurring both teachers and students on to become more involved in the classroom.

The following are some quick and easy ways to practice this skill with beginning teachers.

ACTIVITIES TO PRACTICE THIS SKILL WITH NEW TEACHERS

Enthusiasm is a great skill to have in the teaching profession. Without it, lessons will be mundane, students will be uninvolved, and teachers will be unexcited and lacking in energy. Enthusiasm is a skill that can be practiced and honed with the following activities.

First, after observing enthusiastic teachers and videotaping lessons to look for energy and passion, as mentioned previously, beginning teachers can create lists of the positive tones and activities they observed. Then, by choosing just one new activity a day to practice and implement, beginning teachers can begin growing some new tools and strategies for increasing enthusiasm in their classrooms.

Guiding and helping a pre-service or beginning teacher in how to make a lackluster lesson exciting can also be helpful. Many new curriculum programs contain *scripted* lessons that are sometimes lacking in fun and interest. While teachers are often told to teach such lessons *with fidelity*, there is no reason why a quick introductory or final activity can't be added to spice things up. Giving an existing lesson plan to a pre-service teacher and having them add some spice and interest can be a great way to practice the skill of enthusiasm in the classroom. Not everything in teachers' guides is presented in an exciting way. Assisting a new teacher in how to add some activities can make a huge difference in how the lesson is presented. Sometimes by simply adding a new activity, students will be more involved, and the lesson, more enjoyable.

Another time that enthusiasm can be practiced is during high-stakes testing. As assessment becomes more valuable in school accountability, schools tend to be testing students on a more regular basis. Testing can be uncomfortable and scary for students of all grade levels. A great deal is based on the data and information gleaned from test results, and it can create stress in classrooms. An enthusiastic teacher can do a little extra during the testing periods in his/her school to alleviate some of this pressure. Doing some extra brain breaks, having some silly challenges and simply telling students how much one believes in them can help to break the tension during these challenging times. An enthusiastic teacher will try to build students' self-esteem, and a pre-service teacher can assist in making these testing weeks especially light and more comfortable for students.

Asking the students (depending on the age and grade level) what they like to do and about their interests can also assist a teacher in increasing the participation level in the classroom. An enthusiastic teacher takes time to build relationships, to get to know the students, and to build lessons around the material and events that interest them. Students will be thankful for teachers who take the time to develop meaningful relationships and show that they care about their individual needs. Making connections and creating a sense of community are all key components of passionate and caring teachers who embody a sense of enthusiasm toward the teaching profession as a whole.

In conclusion, teachers who show enthusiasm for their jobs and their students are those who go the extra mile to reach students, teach with interest and compassion, and make even the most mundane lessons exciting. They don't just lecture and give tests; they make connections and meet students' needs. They show spirit and curiosity toward learning, and help children to find meaning in both the lessons they learn and their subsequent pathways into the world.

Enthusiasm in a teacher means that they care enough to do more than what is expected, and that the children in their classrooms are important. A teacher who acts like school is fun and meaningful encourages students to follow their lead, as well. The soft skill of enthusiasm can make or break the school year for students. An enthusiastic teacher will be memorable and make learning unforgettable for his or her students.

KEY IDEAS

- Enthusiasm is contagious. If a teacher teaches with enthusiasm, the students will learn with enthusiasm.
- An enthusiastic teacher makes learning fun and interesting.
- Enthusiastic teachers create lessons that are engaging and motivating.

- Enthusiasm is a skill that can be taught and practiced. Spending time with an enthusiastic teacher can be a great model for beginning teachers.
- Videotaping lessons and watching for both the teacher's enthusiasm and the involvement of the students is a beneficial technique for learning about enthusiasm.
- Enthusiasm and a passion for teaching will help teachers enjoy their job, too.

4

CREATIVITY

- Why is creativity important to beginning teachers?
- How can I model this skill for pre-service and beginning teachers?
- What are some activities that can be used to practice this skill?

IMPORTANCE OF CREATIVITY IN TEACHING

Creativity in teaching is a key soft skill for educators. Creativity involves being imaginative, thinking outside the box, and coming up with original ideas. Creative teachers can make lessons exciting, teach in new and innovative ways, encourage imagination, and inspire children to reach their dreams.

Creative teachers don't just instruct from the book. They come up with imaginative ways to teach the curriculum and cover the content areas. They follow the guidelines and requirements for teaching but do this in ways that are fun, creative, and inventive. They think outside the box and are constantly working to discover new ways to make connections and teach skills that are meaningful to the students in their classroom.

One of the characteristics of excellent teachers is that of creativity, as teachers who are creative make learning fun for students and use activities and strategies that are exciting and adventurous. They also have a mind-set that allows for innovation and originality. In a study of award-winning teachers, Danah Henriksen and Punya Mishra researched the characteristics of outstanding teachers and found the following:

> In reflecting on their beliefs, most of the award-winning teachers noted that creativity was not a generic or detached skill, but a mindset that affects how they see the world. They knew that insights they might have in one area can carry over into new areas of activity. So they maintained open-minded awareness of interesting things in the world around them, looking for innovative ideas for the classroom. (Henriksen and Mishra 2013)

Being open-minded and willing to try new things are great qualities in a teacher and encourages creativity to drive the instruction. It also allows the teacher to create lessons that are meaningful and relevant to the students while teaching in a way that reaches students by providing enthusiasm and interest.

Teachers who work to make content meaningful to students and discover innovative ways to educate them are those that students love to be around. They make rote lessons fun and add some excitement and enthusiasm to their teaching. They use methods like inquiry and cooperative learning, and they allow students to make choices in their learning. These teachers encourage ownership of the classroom and foster the development of a community of learners.

Creativity also incorporates the skill of problem-solving, as it allows students to be innovative, try new things, and use ideas that others may not have discovered. It allows children to see that everything does not have to be done in the same way, and that there are different ways to arrive at an answer.

Promoting the skill of creativity in the classroom can also incorporate a variety of ways to evaluate learning. Using multiple modalities to assess understanding, encouraging children to complete projects to show their mastery of skills, and creating assessments that are varied and authentic are also ways that teachers can be creative in classrooms. Students do not all learn in the same way, so evaluating their knowledge of subject matter can be done in imaginative ways that emphasize their styles of learning.

Instead of taking tests and completing worksheets, students can design and create projects, develop contracts for what they want to know, and work with others to problem-solve and learn new strategies. A creative teacher allows students to think outside the box and *show what they know* in ways other than tests. In brief, creative teachers promote learning in a fun and exciting way. They bring innovative and interesting ideas into the classroom and encourage inquiry and curiosity among students. They teach in ways that are unpredictable and motivating. They also help students learn to foster their own creativity and inspire them to think outside the box.

Creative teachers are an asset to classrooms, as they are motivational and help others see a variety of ways to think and teach. The soft skill of creativity is one that beginning teachers can develop and perfect in their college classes and in their future classrooms.

The following are ways to teach and model this skill for them.

HOW TO MODEL THIS SKILL FOR BEGINNING TEACHERS

College professors and mentor teachers can help to develop the skill of creativity in many ways. First, in college courses, professors can encourage activities which promote creativity and allow students to design projects that are innovative and original. They can provide guidelines for students but allow them to create products that fit their own learning styles and interests.

Universities can also promote creativity by allowing pre-service teachers to write lesson plans that allow for creative pursuits. A professor can assign a standard or content area and allow their college students to be original and innovative in how they go about this. Oftentimes, professors promote only one lesson idea or format, and allowing for creativity can facilitate the options and originality that students use.

Professors can also model creativity in their own teaching. Limiting lectures and repetitive assignments and allowing students to learn the content in new and original ways will model this soft skill for pre-service teachers. Also, encouraging pre-service teachers to use the skill of creativity in lessons with children will encourage the development of this skill.

Mentor teachers can also help to shape creativity in student teachers and practicum students through modeling and encouragement. Classroom teachers teach lessons on a daily basis, and modeling how to make them interesting and creative is a key to teaching this skill to student teachers.

Co-teaching and co-planning can also promote creativity in beginning teachers. By taking a boring lesson plan and revamping it together, the mentor teacher and student teacher can add interest, imagination, and inquiry into an existing lesson. Sometimes just varying a plan or adding an activity can make it more relevant and fun for the children in the classroom.

Taking scripted lessons and curriculum requirements and adding a little spice to them is another way that mentor teachers can model creativity in the classroom. As long as the curriculum is still covered and the administration approves of adapted lessons, student teachers can learn to work within the required elements of teaching while still being innovative.

Planning for a variety of assessments with a beginning teacher is also a great way to model creativity in the classroom. Allowing students to show their learning in a new and different way promotes a variety of learning styles and encourages individuality in the classroom.

Asking students in the class for input about teaching and projects is also beneficial in developing creativity. Since everyone has different interests and passions, trying to involve the children in the planning and learning is a great way to promote creativity for both the teachers and students. The children may come up with some incredible new ways to learn a skill and will enjoy being asked for their opinion.

But what about the pre-service teachers who claim that they just aren't creative? Many people swear that they are not creative and don't know how to be. However, creativity is a skill that can be nurtured and developed in both adults and children. Sometimes encouragement to think outside the box and a willingness to try something different can go a long way for those who believe they are not inventive.

Being creative can also mean that one is resourceful. Not everyone has artistic and imaginative skills, but they can develop their resourcefulness by investigating ideas on the Internet, observing lessons taught by others, and simply trying new things in the classroom. Teachers can develop this skill and learn that resourcefulness and creativity truly do go hand in hand in the classroom.

Overall, the soft skill of creativity is one that can be taught and nurtured in the classroom. Through observation, encouragement, and a little innovation, beginning teachers can develop this skill and see how much it can impact learning in the classroom. Children love teachers who are out of the ordinary and teach lessons that are interesting and fun. Teaching creative lessons can also help teachers break up the monotony of teaching and increase their own passion for their craft. By looking beyond the curriculum and investigating new strategies for learning, a teacher can make a difference in the classroom.

The following section contains some ideas and approaches for accomplishing this goal.

ACTIVITIES TO PRACTICE THIS SKILL WITH NEW TEACHERS

In a recent article, Ashley Lamb-Sinclair (2018) stated that

> Young teachers are in classrooms where it's easy to get bogged down by rules and regulations, but what our students need is our creativity. Teachers shouldn't be afraid to cultivate their own passions and should be open to letting those pursuits guide how they design lessons for students.

This idea is perfect for guiding activities to develop creativity in beginning teachers. All new teachers have passions and interests, and encouraging them to develop these skills in the classroom is a great way to begin teaching creativity. Allowing a beginning teacher to bring his/her strengths and interests into the lessons is also a wonderful way for children to learn about him/her as well.

Permitting practicum students to develop lessons which involve creativity and innovation is also a nice way to encourage this skill in the classroom. Guiding a new teacher through the development of lessons and adding some interest and motivation can help new teachers become independent thinkers and original planners.

Creativity can also be learned by taking mundane lessons and adapting them to add creativity and interest. Although new teachers should be taught to abide by required curriculum and other constraints, they can also be encouraged to add a new idea to a scripted lesson or mandatory lessons. By learning to follow the code of the school system and also adapt plans a bit to add interest, beginning teachers can learn balance in planning and teaching.

Developing different lessons and authentic assessments also helps a new teacher to develop the skill of creativity. Students learn in many ways, and being able to show what they know in a variety of ways is a useful skill for beginning teachers. Learning to think beyond a test is a simple but innovative way to develop creativity in teachers.

In brief, teachers who have the soft skill of creativity make learning fun and interesting for their students. They bring their passions and interests into teaching and develop curiosity and imagination in the students they teach. Creative teachers make sure that the required curriculum is taught but do so in a way that involves children in the learning.

Creative teachers also come to school each day ready to teach and excited about the material they will explain. They use innovation and originality to convey new ideas and explain old strategies. By being creative and doing fun and interesting activities in their classrooms, they will instill a love of learning in their students and avoid the monotony of doing the same thing every day. Creative teachers love learning, and their teaching abilities and passions show this skill in the classroom.

KEY IDEAS

- Creativity involves innovation, passion, interests, and a certain amount of risk-taking for teachers.
- Creativity is *thinking outside the box* while still following the required guidelines for curriculum and planning.
- The skill of creativity can be taught and nurtured in pre-service and beginning teachers.
- Being creative and resourceful go hand in hand. If a teacher does not consider herself creative, she can still be resourceful in her teaching.
- Students who have creative teachers are often more involved in their learning, and will develop the skill of creativity as well.
- Teachers who are creative can make their jobs more fun and will likely have more passion for the education profession.

5

DECISION-MAKING SKILLS

- Why are decision-making skills important to beginning teachers?
- How can I model decision-making skills for beginning teachers?
- What are some activities for practicing decision-making skills?

IMPORTANCE OF DECISION-MAKING SKILLS IN TEACHING

The ability to make decisions is another important disposition needed in teachers. Being able to make clear decisions at a moment's notice is vital for classroom success. Teachers, regardless of grade level, make a number of decisions each day—from how to teach the information in lessons to which child to call on for a response, and even what color of background paper to use for a bulletin board. These decisions are often spontaneous, with little time to make careful selections or reflect on one's decisions.

Teachers need to be able to make decisions quickly, focusing on what is best for the children in their classrooms as well as for the curriculum they are teaching. These are the important, *think on one's feet* decisions that occur daily in classrooms, and the sheer number of them can be daunting. In fact, research by Philip Johnson (1990) reveals that "the average classroom teacher [makes] 1,500 decisions a day"

(*Life in Classrooms*, 149). Making that many decisions in a day can be tiring, and represents a huge amount of responsibility for a new teacher.

Knowing how to handle decision-making in a quick, yet appropriate, way is important for all teachers, but especially those with little experience. The ability to make rapid yet accurate decisions is vital to the success of beginning teachers. When children misbehave or a fire alarm goes off, teachers do not have minutes to make decisions—they have mere seconds to respond to the situation and make decisions that will impact the safety and well-being of children.

Although decision-making is an important soft skill in the teaching profession, impacting all areas of the school day, it is often not part of the instruction in college courses. Decision-making needs to be practiced and taught in a variety of ways to help prepare future teachers for the quick choices they will need to make, and to ensure that the children they are teaching are prepared and ready as well. By being able to make a change or judgment at a moment's notice, beginning teachers will be equipped for the many deviations that occur in a typical school day.

This soft skill is also important in the integral parts of teaching, such as planning, instructing, and behavior management. Each day, teachers must decide which content to teach and how to handle misbehaviors in the classroom. They need to know which strategies to use and what to do when children do not comprehend lessons. Being able to make an unplanned shift in their teaching to accommodate learners is key to aiding in the successful development and understanding of students.

By learning about decision-making in college classrooms and field experiences, pre-service teachers will be better able to handle the quick decisions that impact curriculum and teaching, as well. They will be able to relate to individual students and make decisions that are appropriate for each child in their classroom. In most college courses, future teachers are taught to plan lessons, create assessments, and correct misbehaviors in children. They are taught the importance of curriculum and standards, and how to differentiate for the needs of their students. However, the soft skill of decision-making is often hard to teach; it has to happen quickly, and it's hard to learn in a college lecture. Practicing for the unknown and learning to *wing it* on occasion can help prepare future teachers to use this skill in the classroom.

The following section will describe ways to teach and model decision-making in real-world environments, along with activities for practicing this skill.

HOW TO MODEL THESE SKILLS FOR BEGINNING TEACHERS

Some element of decision-making happens at every moment in a classroom setting. Teachers constantly have to decide which behaviors to address or ignore, what skills are necessary to teach the required curriculum, and how to think quickly in emergency situations. There is no *textbook answer* for what is right and how to proceed. Much of this skill is learned in teacher-education classes and in practicum settings, such as student teaching. However, one of the best ways to learn this skill is through reflective observation and conversation.

In practicum and field-based education classes, explaining why certain decisions are made by veteran teachers can be highly effective. For example, if a teacher does not call on a particular student for answers, it may be because the teacher knows about a situation or difficulty that child may be experiencing at home. Learning the reasons that a teacher makes this decision can be insightful to beginning teachers. In a quick observation, it is difficult to understand the choices made by the classroom teacher, so having conversations with new teachers can be very helpful in this regard.

On the same issue, it is important to encourage new teachers to ask questions about why certain decisions were made. When a child is exhibiting attention-seeking behaviors, such as yelling out or acting silly, sometimes the most effective way to handle it is to simply ignore the behavior. A rookie teacher may not understand that this was indeed a conscious effort on the part of the veteran teacher to not draw more attention to the student at hand. Being allowed to ask why teachers chose to handle certain situations the way they did can create wonderful dialogue, if the questions are asked in a respectful and kind way. Remembering to ask, "I wonder why . . . ?" types of questions as opposed to challenging a veteran teacher is an important skill for all beginning teachers to learn.

Asking these kinds of questions and having intentional conversations about why teachers make certain decisions over others can help preservice and new teachers learn more about the real-world decision-making process that takes place in classrooms every day. While there is never one absolutely correct answer to each dilemma teachers face, working through situations and finding out how veteran teachers make the decisions they do can be very helpful.

Another way that veteran teachers can model decision-making behaviors is to simply respond with "What do *you* think?" when a student teacher asks a question. Often, mentor teachers answer questions from students or new teachers without having them reflect on the situation at hand. Instead of providing direct answers, asking questions can provide more insight and growth for new teachers.

For example, if a child is misbehaving in the classroom, instead of providing solutions to a beginning teacher, asking the question, "What would you do in your own classroom?" forces student teachers to think about the situation and do some simple decision-making of their own, on the spot. Of course, if that decision is inappropriate, a mentor teacher should chime in, but frequently, new teachers are very capable of coming up with solutions on their own. They simply need affirmation from a veteran teacher that they are on the right track!

An additional strategy to teach and model decision-making skills in the classroom is through co-teaching. In a co-teaching situation, student teachers and mentor teachers work together in an intentional way to co-plan, co-teach, and co-assess the students in their classrooms. They work together in the decision-making process, with the mentor teacher far more involved than the *sink-or-swim* context that was formerly used in student teaching. If student teachers and mentor teachers work together in all aspects of teaching, the modeling of decision-making skills should become almost automatic. As student teachers plan and teach with their mentor teacher, they can ask questions, learn planning techniques, and make decisions together about how to create effective instruction in the classroom. This mentoring is vital in helping a preservice or beginning teacher learn how teachers use decision-making skills on a daily basis.

Being involved with schoolwide and grade-level/subject-area teams is also an important part of decision-making, especially for student teachers and beginning teachers. As more and more collaboration is used in schools, learning the skill of decision-making in a group setting becomes even more valuable. If student teachers and beginning teachers are treated as equals in the decision-making process in grade-level or subject-area teams, they will be more likely to participate and feel that their choices and input are valued by the other group members.

Also, new teachers can provide fresh ideas and teaching methods that can be shared with others. Oftentimes, the enthusiasm and strategies shared by beginning teachers can help to create new and different ideas for use in the classroom, a benefit to mentor teachers and others who guide and assist beginning teachers.

Another way to model decision-making is to allow the students some input into the choices made in the classroom. Although teachers have allowed students to provide input into the development of classroom rules and procedures for decades, having beginning teachers witness and participate in this process is a valuable learning experience. Also, in upper grades, including the students in the decision-making process and allowing a variety of opinions creates a sense of ownership and community within the classroom.

Asking students for their input on projects, including them in problems and concerns that happen in the classroom, and valuing their ideas as citizens of the classroom not only models the soft skill of decision-making but also shows how to include and involve all students in the learning that is taking place.

ACTIVITIES TO PRACTICE THESE SKILLS WITH NEW TEACHERS

A variety of activities for teaching decision-making skills can be used in college classrooms and with beginning teachers. One of the first includes using scenario-based activities with open-ended questions. For example, if the class is studying classroom management techniques, providing the college students with scenarios about situations that involve particular misbehaviors and having them make decisions about how to handle them, either alone or in groups, can be very helpful. Although the best way to learn this soft skill is by making real decisions in the classroom, this opportunity may not always be available. By practicing through scenario-based situations, pre-service teachers can make decisions, brainstorm ideas, and receive feedback on their decisions in the college classroom.

Another way to practice decision-making skills is to view real-world videos of teachers who have a problem, whether with a student's behavior or anything else taught in the classroom. Many videos are available through the Internet that allow the viewer to watch a videotaped scenario and then stop and pause the tape in order to discuss ways to solve the problem at hand. Encouraging pre-service teachers to watch these videos and reflect on ways to solve the classroom problems portrayed can help them learn from other situations and hopefully apply these skills in their future classrooms. Also, reflecting as a class on why the teachers in the videos made the decisions they did will allow helpful discussion and analysis that will assist in future decision-making.

Practicing open-ended job interview questions can also assist with decision-making skills. Employers today frequently use open-ended, scenario-based questions for teacher interviews. The interviewer may present a particular problem or issue in a classroom and then ask the teacher applicant to explain what they would do in that situation. Being able to practice these scenarios is beneficial and can be accomplished either in a college classroom or in a career center, available on most college campuses.

Along with open-ended scenarios in teacher interviews, scenario-based questions are also being used more on teacher licensing exams. While these exams have been around for many years, the use of scenario-based questions is becoming more common as an assessment tool. Many testing companies now use this technique to judge the pedagogical knowledge of future teachers, in addition to the content knowledge they also need for future classroom teaching. Being able to see and recognize how to solve the problems that are often asked on teaching exams will also allow pre-service teachers to practice the soft skill of decision-making.

Decision-making skills may also be practiced by having pre-service teachers participate in situations that are often unplanned or emergency-oriented. Assuming that the pre-service teacher is allowed to be alone in the classroom with children (meaning, that appropriate background checks and liability issues are in place), having them *jump in* to cover a situation can be very meaningful.

For example, if the mentor teacher needs to leave the room for a few minutes to assist an ill child, putting the student teacher in charge can help to encourage the decision-making process. While this idea should not be used on the very first visit, an occasional emergency takeover by a student teacher can provide much-needed experience in how to make decisions without the teacher in the room.

In brief, the soft skill of decision-making is often learned during the course of unplanned events that require unexpected decisions. By being able to make quick choices, think on one's feet, and be aware of children's needs and safety issues, pre-service and new teachers will learn how to resolve problems and create solutions that will enable instruction to continue, even in the most unforeseen situations.

KEY IDEAS

- Decision-making skills are important to ensure the safety and well-being of children.
- Decision-making skills are difficult to learn by reading a textbook; they need to be practiced, and are learned by experience.
- New teachers need to hone these skills, as they will often be required to make decisions quickly and spontaneously.
- Allowing pre-service teachers and beginning teachers to participate in decision-making is a great idea for developing this skill.
- Co-teaching and co-planning are wonderful ways to develop the skill of decision-making in the classroom.
- Decision-making skills are often assessed in interview questions and licensing exams and are therefore important to practice before entering the teaching profession.

6

TEAMWORK AND COLLABORATION

- Why is teamwork important for beginning teachers?
- How can I teach and model collaboration skills?
- What are some ideas for practicing this skill with pre-service and beginning teachers?

IMPORTANCE OF TEAMWORK AND COLLABORATION IN TEACHING

Teamwork and collaboration are important skills for new and beginning teachers. As more schools move to a collaborative model of teaching, knowing how to work with others and use cooperative learning is an essential soft skill. Many schools incorporate the use of team planning and co-teaching, and being able to adjust to this type of teaching is vital to today's beginning teachers.

According to the Association for Teacher Educators (ATE), "Accomplished teacher educators adopt a collaborative approach to teacher education that involves a variety of stakeholders (e.g., universities, schools, families, communities, foundations, businesses, and museums) in teaching and learning" (ATE 2018). Being able to work with others, including colleagues and families, is an important soft skill for working in today's schools.

Grade-level teams in elementary schools and subject-level departments in upper grades are a critical part of teaching today, and knowing how to work with others can make or break one's success in the first year of teaching. Being able to contribute to a team approach of teaching while also knowing one's place as a pre-service or beginning teacher is key to effective teamwork. Remembering to honor the experience and expertise of veteran teachers while working with the teaching team is a crucial part of being accepted by other teachers in the building. Being humble and approachable is one of the most important parts of this soft skill.

Another important part of teamwork and collaboration is being aware of the workload and dividing it appropriately. Making sure that pre-service and beginning teachers are part of the school team is important, and this goes for sharing the workload as well. If each teacher is supposed to contribute to a teaching unit, for example, then completing the work in a timely manner is crucial. Developing a sense of teamwork makes all teachers' jobs easier. By dividing the workload, covering for another teacher in an emergency, and being able to call a colleague when one is ill, teachers can work together and help in all parts of the school day. By being a *team player*, other staff members in the building are more likely to help and show empathy when a new teacher needs it.

Sharing one's strengths and weaknesses with others can also be a big part of teamwork and collaboration. Knowing who on the grade-level team is great at classroom management or creative teaching strategies is important. Also, being able to share one's own strengths is helpful to a beginning teacher. Often, beginning teachers bring important skills, like how to use new technology, along with fresh enthusiasm that invigorates the team in ways that veteran teachers appreciate.

Collaboration is also noticed by the children in the classroom. Students notice who works well together and who doesn't, even though they are adults. Modeling the skill of teamwork with colleagues and others in the school can also show children how to appropriately work with others. Knowing how to work together as a team and modeling the appropriate skills of collaboration are important for teachers to use in their classrooms. The soft skill of working together is one that is necessary in today's schools; the phrase *It takes a village to raise a child* is indeed true. One teacher alone may not be able to complete all teaching tasks, but several teachers with the same goal in mind will accomplish much more! In conclusion, teamwork and collaboration are vital to the success of beginning teachers. Knowing when to share and when to seek help from others can truly benefit them as they begin their teaching careers.

The following are some ideas for how to teach and model ideas for teamwork in college courses or school classrooms.

HOW TO MODEL THESE SKILLS FOR BEGINNING TEACHERS

Teaching and modeling appropriate collaboration and teamwork skills is a crucial role for mentor teachers. Being able to show beginning teachers how to work with others and collaborate for the sake of children is a soft skill that will always be needed. Providing opportunities to do this can happen in the following ways.

First, welcoming a student teacher or beginning teacher into the classroom or grade level is a vital step in modeling teamwork in schools. Offering to help with questions, being there to provide helpful advice, and providing encouragement to new teachers is a way to open the door to teamwork. Often, new teachers are reluctant to ask for help, as they do not want to admit their weaknesses. However, knowing that a supportive teacher is nearby is a beginning step for collaboration.

Co-teaching is also a helpful approach to mentoring new teachers in the area of teamwork. Co-teaching has been used in the area of special education for many years, but the idea of working with more than one teacher in the classroom is becoming more popular in other areas as well. The strategy of co-teaching can also be used with paraprofessionals but needs to be implemented carefully and intentionally so that all adults in the room are working together to achieve a common goal.

Involving new teachers in committee work, collaborative planning, and school-based programs is another great way to teach and model teamwork. While it is important to not recruit new teachers for every project during their first year, it's critical to invite them to see the inner workings of committees, and the school as a whole. Involving student teachers as well makes them feel welcome and respected by their teaching colleagues.

Another important part of teamwork is learning to work with difficult people. Unfortunately, there are difficult teachers and negative attitudes in every school. Sometimes, teachers are simply overwhelmed, and other times they may have a lot to deal with outside of the classroom. Modeling how to deal with difficult people is also a skill that mentor teachers can use with beginning teachers. Sometimes, modeling a kind word or action can do a great deal to help build rapport with the negative people in a school. Other times, learning the skill of redirection can be successful. When someone begins to complain, redirecting the conversation to something more positive can make a huge difference in how teamwork evolves in a school.

In addition, learning that there are simply some topics that a new teacher should avoid is a great skill for mentors to model in the classroom. Politics, religion, and anything controversial to the school should be avoided if at all possible. If the school is in the middle of a contract dispute, for example, learning that it's not wise to bring up this topic can be helpful to new teachers.

In brief, modeling collaboration skills and teamwork is a very important task for a mentor teacher to complete. As pre-service and beginning teachers enter the teaching profession, it is crucial for them to see respectful relationships among teachers and to know the skills it takes to work well with others and avoid conflict.

The next section will include ideas for teaching teamwork and collaboration, whether in teacher-preparation classes or in the school setting. These ideas are easy to implement and will help pre-service teachers learn to collaborate and become effective team members in a school environment.

ACTIVITIES TO PRACTICE THESE SKILLS WITH NEW TEACHERS

Many things can be done to teach teamwork and collaboration in the classroom. First, new teachers can use icebreakers and introductory activities during the first few weeks of school to get to know his/her students and convey a sense of community in the classroom. If a teacher cares enough to build relationships with his/her students, the children are more likely to participate in team activities later in the school year.

Another technique for teaching collaboration is the use of cooperative learning. This skill could be used in college courses to model for pre-service teachers how to effectively work together. It could also be used in classrooms with children who are learning the techniques of cooperative learning, including the social skills necessary to work with others.

Collaborative projects, whether in college classes or in a school setting, are also important for teaching the skill of teamwork. However, it's key to remember that collaborative projects involve more than just throwing people into groups to work together. Explaining and teaching techniques of collaboration, allowing class or school time to complete projects, and holding all members of the group accountable for their work can teach this skill to pre-service teachers before they enter the teaching profession.

Working on team-building activities at faculty retreats or beginning-of-the-year meetings is also a good way to teach and model collaboration and teamwork for all teachers. The start of the school year can be hectic, but allowing time for new faculty members and student teachers in the building to get to know others can be beneficial in creating a sense of collaboration in the school. A few simple activities, such as introductions and icebreakers for faculty members, can be important ways to encourage this teamwork.

Also, it may seem simple, but it's important to ensure that new student teachers or beginning teachers take the time to introduce themselves, or be introduced to others in the building, and to learn to work with these faculty members in a respectful way. Being introduced to other staff members in the building, including secretaries, custodians, the school nurse, and cafeteria workers also creates a sense of teamwork and collaboration in a school. All of these employees play an important role in schools, but are often overlooked in the introduction process.

It has become increasingly important for teachers to learn to work with others and use the skills of collaboration and teamwork before appearing in their own classrooms. More schools are using a team-teaching approach or a subject-area department, so knowing how to be a team player is even more vital in today's classrooms. Co-planning and co-teaching in both pre-service education classes and in student teaching will model how to appropriately do this in the real world.

Another idea for teaching teamwork involves a simple discussion of the importance of working together versus working alone. Working together can model the appropriate skills of collaboration for future classrooms. It can lighten the workload when teams divide the curriculum among themselves, and model collaboration skills for children in the classroom when they see the adults around them working together positively in co-teaching situations.

Learning to be a team player and effectively working with others in a teaching situation is a soft skill that needs to be modeled and practiced so that pre-service and beginning teachers can realize the importance of this skill as well as ways to effectively implement it during their first years of teaching. It may not be easy to collaborate with all of the people one encounters, but learning some positive ways to interact can help one go far in the teaching profession.

Also, as schools move to a more collaborative approach to education, the idea of teamwork is being addressed more often in interviews and job selection. Schools and administrators are increasingly aware of the importance of this skill when hiring new teachers. An interview question currently being used in school corporations focuses on whether a prospective teacher works better alone or in a group. Being able to answer this question honestly, with examples of ways one has used collaboration and teamwork in their teacher preparation, can be a very important skill for many, and may just make the difference in getting the job.

In conclusion, teamwork and collaboration are vital to the success of beginning teachers in today's world of team teaching and cooperation. Teachers who are able to work together to accomplish goals, plan lessons, and model collaboration skills for their students are educators who can implement a successful learning environment for the entire school.

KEY IDEAS

- Teamwork and collaboration are important parts of the teaching profession, increasingly being used in grade-level teams and subject-area units.
- Collaborative projects in college courses model the significance of teamwork in teaching.
- Working with colleagues and doing one's share of the work are necessary skills in collaboration.

- Learning to work with difficult colleagues is a key part of this soft skill, and needs to be modeled by mentor teachers.
- Modeling appropriate teamwork is vital for the teacher, as students see the teacher's example in working with others.
- Emphasizing the importance of co-teaching and collaboration in teaching is important for future teachers.

7

STRESS MANAGEMENT

- Why is stress management important for beginning teachers?
- How can I teach and model stress-management skills?
- What are some activities for teaching this skill to pre-service and beginning teachers?

IMPORTANCE OF STRESS MANAGEMENT IN TEACHING

It goes without saying that teaching can be a stressful job. Demands from administrators and parents and issues with classroom management can be overwhelming to beginning teachers. In addition, state testing requirements, teaching evaluations, and other mandates of the profession add even more stress. Learning how to deal with the requirements of teaching, while maintaining a healthy lifestyle and a lower stress level, is a soft skill that all teachers need.

An article in *NEA Today* about work-related stress addresses this topic:

> According to the Bureau of Labor Statistics, 75 percent of Americans say their jobs are stressful. But what a lot of educators experience isn't the everyday variety of workplace tension. It's nerve-jangling, sleep-robbing, heart-pounding stress that comes from all directions and can leave them constantly anxious and fatigued. (NEA 2012)

Being able to handle *teacher stress* is a valuable skill for those entering the education field. While stress is a part of daily life, in the teaching profession it is important to keep stress levels at a minimum. Being able to monitor stress levels and teach in a calm and caring way is not only important for the mental health of the teacher but for the children in the classroom as well. Knowing that one's mood and behaviors can directly impact one's teaching and interactions with children and others is an important reason to make sure that stress is addressed during the course of teacher training.

The saying *Never let them see you sweat* is key to remember when handling stress levels in a school setting. Children, whether preschool age or adolescents, can tell when a teacher feels stressed. A teacher has certain facial expressions, body language, and even words that come across in a different way when he or she is feeling stressed. This stress in turn can be passed on to students, thereby multiplying the stress level in the situation.

Knowing that stress can impact not only the teacher but others as well is a reason to maintain a healthy stress level in the teaching profession. A high level of stress can lead teachers to make inappropriate decisions in teaching, which has a ripple effect on the children. Students will mirror the actions of a teacher who comes across as calm and collected, and hopefully this will lead to the same mood in the classroom environment. By the same token, if children sense a stressful environment, they will likely mirror this in their behavior and actions in the classroom.

Stress can also impact the well-being, both physical and mental, of beginning teachers. Stress can lead to health problems, decreased attendance at school, and lower productivity in the classroom. It can also lead to less sleep, increased anxiety, and more fragility in a new teacher. Since teachers already have enough on their plates, it is important for them to learn stress management to deter these issues in the future.

Knowing ways to handle stress, learning how to take care of oneself, and being able to ask for help when needed are all ways that beginning teachers can reduce the level of stress in their lives as well as in their classrooms. A stressful environment creates a negative experience for everyone who enters, and being aware of ways to create stress-free learning spaces for both children and adults is indeed a beneficial life skill. Being aware of one's stress levels and finding ways to cope with the stress involved in teaching is important to teach and model to pre-service and beginning teachers. The following will address ways to model this important skill.

HOW TO MODEL THIS SKILL FOR BEGINNING TEACHERS

An old proverb says *Imitation is the sincerest form of flattery*. One of the first things that mentor teachers, professors, and administrators can do to help with stress management is to remember that others are always watching. Pre-service and beginning teachers often look to their mentors to see how they handle stressful and difficult situations. Simply modeling calm and composed reactions to problems is one of the best things a mentor teacher can do.

Another way to teach about stress management is to share one's thoughts and ideas with pre-service and beginning teachers when a difficult situation occurs. For example, when a child misbehaves or the necessary technology does not work, having a conversation in private with the new teacher can be very effective. Saying, "When Samantha was throwing a fit, I was very upset. However, I knew that if I yelled back or made a big deal about the behavior, it would escalate even more," can help a rookie teacher see that while teachers are indeed human, the decisions they make can impact the entire classroom environment. Sharing these *teachable moments* with beginning teachers is effective and impactful in the learning process of the classroom. When mentor teachers think aloud and provide explanations for the decisions they make—especially when these choices decrease the stress in a situation—it's a valuable teaching tool indeed.

Another way to model stress management in the classroom is by sharing with mentees how one handles personal stress, both in- and outside of school. Sharing real-life situations with others, such as how one juggles a full-time job, parenthood, and other life responsibilities, can help teach pre-service students the stress-management techniques of multitasking and prioritizing. Modeling these skills shows that it is possible to do multiple tasks at once while minimizing the stress level in the classroom.

It is also important for mentor teachers to model the idea of *self-care* for beginning teachers. Encouraging them to have a life outside the classroom and being involved in hobbies and interests can do a great deal to lessen stress levels. Going for a run, reading a book for pleasure, watching a favorite television show, or simply doing nothing are all important ideas to share with new teachers, as this models the fact that self-care is important in every profession.

Stress-management techniques, including deep breathing, visualization, and calming techniques, are also wonderful strategies to model for beginning teachers. Sometimes during a stressful day, simply taking a deep breath and a quick break from the action can deescalate the chaos in the classroom, and can be used by both the teacher and the students. Ideas like *brain breaks* in the middle of a stressful situation can help both groups calm down and continue the lesson in a more meaningful manner.

Though stress can be managed in several quick and effortless ways, like deep breathing or brain breaks, it is also important to address the fact that sometimes, managing stress requires more than just simple strategies in the classroom. Remember that asking for help is a valid technique in stress management, whether it's seeking advice from a teacher or administrator, or getting professional help. It's important for beginning teachers to understand that stress is a very real part of teaching, but if it becomes overwhelming, there is help available.

Modeling how one handles stress can be one of the most important parts of being a mentor teacher to pre-service and beginning teachers. Showing new teachers that one has emotions, and often feels the stress of teaching, can turn into a teachable moment in the classroom. Talking aloud about how one deals with stressful situations without losing one's cool is an important skill to model and share with all new teachers.

The next section will address some simple ideas for stress management for new teachers, and focuses on ways to both teach and use stress-management tools when working with children. By learning and modeling this skill to beginning teachers, they will learn that although stress is inevitable in the teaching profession, management skills will indeed help.

STRESS MANAGEMENT

ACTIVITIES TO PRACTICE THIS SKILL WITH NEW TEACHERS

As stated above, a certain level of stress is a part of teaching in the classroom. However, if teachers let the stress get to them, changing their mood and actions, it can be unhealthy and unwelcome in the classroom. The following are some ideas for how to teach stress management in the classroom.

Children and students enter the classroom each day with varying levels of stress. They may have had a rough morning, forgotten their homework, or had other issues that disrupted their normal routine. However, when a teacher welcomes students each morning with a smile and and a hug, handshake, or a high five, it can start the day off in a good way. Knowing that a caring teacher is in charge can do a great deal to eliminate the stress that children may bring with them into the classroom. Sometimes just starting the day in a positive way can make a huge difference, for both the children and the teacher.

Community circles and morning meetings can also be used to get the morning off to a smooth start. Gathering students at the beginning of the day or class period and doing a quick check-in about events of the day, concerns about assignments, and other topics on the minds of children can start the day in a stress-free way, which of course will rub off on the teacher as well.

Teaching relaxation skills to children can also be used to reduce the stress level of the teacher. Often, something as simple as deep breathing or putting one's head down for a minute can lessen the stress level, too. Encouraging new teachers to use these techniques in addition to brain breaks and other stress-reducing activities can help to lower the stress levels in their classrooms.

Another skill that can help in the classroom is the the idea of teaching procedures, routines, and other processes to the students in advance. For example, making sure that both new teachers and their students know the proper procedure for a fire drill can help to alleviate the stress of an unknown situation. Having routines in place can lead to a calmer environment simply because they create a level of safety and security in today's classrooms.

Teaching pre-service and beginning teachers the importance of organization can also help with stress reduction. Everyone has had a day when he/she overslept, had a flat tire, or was stuck in a traffic jam on the way to work. However, arriving late to a well-organized, clean, and orderly classroom can help to improve a stressful day. Also, knowing that lesson plans are ready and materials are prepared will help start the morning off with less stress than entering a disorganized and unplanned classroom.

Other ways to help pre-service and new teachers with the soft skill of stress management include working ahead on required projects or plans, communicating and collaborating with others, and maintaining a work schedule that is healthy and productive. It is common for beginning teachers to spend many hours after school preparing and planning for future lessons; however, new teachers also need to share the workload and take time for themselves, as well.

Another important part of teaching is remembering that it is acceptable to ask for help. New teachers need to know that seeking the advice of a mentor teacher or a person who has understanding and empathy can be helpful, as veteran teachers usually have good advice and have often been in the same situations. With the benefit of this advice, beginning teachers will learn how to handle difficult situations in more appropriate ways the next time they happen.

In brief, stress is found in every teaching position. Learning to manage one's stress in a healthy way is a very important soft skill for beginning teachers. Being able to talk with veteran teachers, using stress-reduction techniques in the classroom, and learning the importance of taking time for oneself are all part of helping new teachers enter the profession.

The faster a teacher can learn this skill, the more likely he/she will be able to manage stress in a teaching job and confront the various stressors that come with this profession. If a teacher can learn to deal with stress at an early stage in his/her career, it is more likely that he/she can work through the burnout that often comes in later years. By having a positive attitude and the coping skills to deal with stress, beginning teachers are more likely to be successful for many years to come.

KEY IDEAS

- Teaching is a stressful job. Knowing how to handle stressful situations is vital to the success of beginning teachers.
- Learning how to remain calm in stressful conditions is important to model with students, as it sets the tone for the classroom.
- It is essential for mentor teachers to discuss and model how to handle stressful situations with pre-service and beginning teachers.
- Practicing self-care is critical for beginning teachers, as stress can lead to both medical and psychological issues.
- Being organized and prepared can help to alleviate stress in beginning teachers.
- Having a positive attitude is essential to reducing stress in the classroom.

8

POSITIVE ATTITUDE

- Why is a positive attitude important in teaching?
- How can I model a positive attitude to new educators?
- What are some activities to practice this skill with pre-service and beginning teachers?

IMPORTANCE OF A POSITIVE ATTITUDE IN TEACHING

Although it seems pretty obvious, having a positive attitude can make or break a teacher's day as well as that of the students in the classroom. Being positive, even in the worst situations, not only helps the teacher maintain a positive demeanor but also helps the students learn how to be positive as well.

Imagine that your alarm doesn't go off, your car doesn't start, or there's a traffic jam on your usual route to school. It can happen to anyone at any time, but how one chooses to deal with it will determine what happens next. Being positive and remaining calm will not only help the teacher but anyone else he/she encounters during the day.

Having a passion for one's vocation is one of the best assets a teacher can have, and having an affirming, positive attitude is contagious. If the teacher wants to be there, so will the students. Everyone has had a teacher with a negative attitude, and that attitude can spread among students. According to Robert Marzano, author of *The Highly Engaged Classroom*, "The most general influence on a student's emotional engagement is a teacher's positive demeanor. A teacher can communicate a positive demeanor through demonstrating enthusiasm and intensity, both of which have been associated with student engagement and achievement" (Marzano 2010).

If a student perceives a positive attitude from his teacher, he will be far more likely to participate, more willing to listen, and more likely to have proper classroom behavior. Noticing when children are doing the right thing and praising appropriate behaviors can go far in promoting a positive attitude in the classroom. A simple "I love that Group One has their materials out and is ready for the next lesson" goes a long way toward setting a positive classroom environment.

Learning to *catch students being good* and praising appropriate behavior is an important skill for beginning teachers. Instead of nagging about inappropriate behaviors, a teacher who notices good behavior is likely to have better relationships with students and better classroom management than one who yells and only notices when a student is not behaving properly. Providing appropriate praise and feedback is also a vital part of a positive attitude. Giving genuine praise when a student is doing well—and providing encouragement for those who are struggling—can help to create a positive environment and motivate students to learn, ultimately making the classroom a much happier place.

Another aspect of having a positive attitude is surrounding oneself with positive people. If a new teacher is engulfed in a climate of positive learning and great attitudes, she is likely to continue in the same manner. However, if she is surrounded by negativity, this too will probably impact her attitude and the learning of her students. Learning to seek out a positive environment for teaching and positive colleagues to surround oneself with is a key component of having a positive attitude for teaching, and an important skill to teach beginning educators. A positive attitude is contagious, and being with positive teachers will enable new teachers to develop this skill for the future.

Overall, a positive attitude is a necessary soft skill in the teaching profession. By being positive, teachers create learning environments that are encouraging and inclusive. Positivity also means that teachers will be able to take their own bad days and turn them around, making them more upbeat and constructive.

The following section offers some ways to teach and model a positive attitude in the classroom.

HOW TO MODEL THIS SKILL FOR BEGINNING TEACHERS

Modeling a positive attitude is important for both college instructors and classroom mentors. As with any job, the teaching profession has both good days and bad. However, if a mentor teacher models positivity, it can make all the difference in how a beginning teacher will handle challenges in his/her future classroom.

One of the most important parts of modeling a positive attitude for beginning teachers is creating a positive environment in the classroom. Having a bright and cheerful classroom, being approachable, and setting the tone for learning are all important items to model. Starting each day with a smile on one's face, being prepared and ready, and allowing students who had a rough time the day before to have a fresh start today are all important parts of modeling a positive attitude. Teachers who hold grudges, bring up past behaviors, and remind students of their mistakes will most likely not create environments of positive learning for their students.

Modeling how to build meaningful relationships with students is also a great skill to show beginning teachers. Starting each day off with a kind comment, a morning meeting, or even just greeting students at the door can create relationships with students that will hopefully lead to positive demeanors in the classroom.

Another way to model a positive attitude is to demonstrate appropriate behaviors in front of pre-service and beginning teachers. While mentor teachers are human and will have difficult days, the ways they react to misbehaviors, changes in schedule, and school politics are constantly being observed by student teachers and others new to the profession. Being able to move on, say a positive comment, and keep smiling is a skill that all teachers need to have in order to be successful in the classroom.

Showing beginning teachers how to handle misbehaviors and mistakes in a kind and caring way will also help everyone involved to be more positive. Students misbehave; it's part of teaching. However, the way a teacher handles the misbehavior is vital to maintaining positive relationships and a caring climate for learning. If a preschool teacher yells at a child, or a high school teacher embarrasses a student, the trust and positive relationships will diminish and impact the entire class.

Young teachers are impressionable, and it's important to make an effort to promote the profession of education. Sometimes, veteran teachers are tempted to make negative comments about being a teacher, or complain about the workload, the salaries, or the administration. However, keeping those comments to oneself and not sharing them with new teachers will help to create a more optimistic attitude toward the teaching profession.

In all, a positive attitude is an essential skill for beginning teachers to learn, and mentor teachers to model. By being positive, teachers can have an amazing impact on students and instill positivity in them as well. By creating positive learning environments where children are allowed to make mistakes and misbehaviors are handled in calm and caring ways, teachers can model this skill for new teachers and promote positive classrooms in the future.

ACTIVITIES TO PRACTICE THIS SKILL WITH NEW TEACHERS

There are many ways to promote a positive attitude and caring classroom environment. The first would be creating a positive classroom from the first day of school. Greeting students at the door, welcoming them into the classroom, and providing a safe and inclusive environment for learning are all great ways to set the tone at the beginning of the school year. Doing icebreakers and building relationships with students are also positive ways to get to know the children one is teaching. Asking questions, finding out likes and dislikes, and doing team-building activities all contribute to a positive classroom and a caring environment. Allowing a practicum or student teacher to begin this relationship-building will help to generate a positive attitude, and will enable them to learn skills that will be needed in future classrooms.

Reviewing safety procedures, teaching anti-bullying activities, and going over rules in a positive way will also create a more encouraging environment for learning. By having a sense of order and making students feel safe, the teacher can create a kind and caring classroom, and the children will be more positive as a result.

Modeling how to handle bad days and unexpected events can also help new and beginning teachers. Asking them how they would handle certain situations, and brainstorming about ways that a circumstance might have been handled better in the future, will also expose new teachers to coping strategies for their future classrooms. By having these coping skills, they will be able to practice positivity with students under the caring guidance of a mentor teacher.

Teaching pre-service teachers how to handle negative people and work constructively with grade-level teams or subject-area groups is also a useful activity for future teachers. Simply talking to a new teacher about a comment that was made by an administrator, or discussing how one deals with negative attitudes from others, is a vital skill that can be modeled and addressed by mentor teachers.

Having pre-service teachers or student teachers assist with comments for report cards is another way to teach the idea of positivity. Modeling the idea of starting with a positive comment followed by other remarks is a great way to show beginning teachers that every student has something good in them, and promotes a caring demeanor to parents who read them.

Modeling positive behaviors with parents and families is also important for beginning teachers to see. Parents can sometimes be upset or angry, and showing a new teacher how to talk to parents in a calm and respectful manner is another way to model a positive attitude in the classroom.

Creating goals for individual lessons and future teaching units can instill positivity in lessons. If the goals include positive aspects and clear learning goals, a pre-service teacher is more likely to take the time to teach content in meaningful ways as well as reflect on the positive aspects of teaching.

Modeling positive classroom behaviors with children, such as kindness, empathy, and good manners, will be helpful in creating positive classroom environments as well. Children who are taught to be pleasant and use good manners—saying *please* and *thank you*—go a long way toward promoting a successful classroom community.

Teaching the skills of being positive to children through a predetermined curriculum is another way that a mentor teacher can model positivity in the classroom. Programs such as those outlined in *Mindset* by Carol Dweck (2007), *How Full Is Your Bucket?* (2004) by Tom Rath and Donald Clifton (for older students), and *Have You Filled a Bucket Today?* by Carol McCloud (2015) (for younger children), are great ways to teach children how to have a positive attitude. By creating positive relationships and growth mind-sets, children will also learn the importance of being positive.

For many students in today's classrooms, life at home may not be the most affirming place. Parents may be unavailable, communities may be unsafe, and the responsibilities that families face may seem unbearable. However, a caring teacher who practices positivity in the classroom will be able to help counteract these negative influences and make a difference for years to come.

A teacher's demeanor and attitude determines how the children will react, how the classroom will run, and the behaviors of the classroom in general. Teachers who are negative promote negative environments, but teachers who are positive create warm and caring classrooms where students feel safe, important, and ready to learn.

The soft skill of a positive attitude is important for mentor teachers to model and for pre-service and beginning teachers to learn. The teaching profession is one that can last for decades; walking into a positive classroom each day will make those years zoom by!

KEY IDEAS

- A positive attitude is contagious, and can impact the outlook of the entire class.
- A teacher's positive demeanor is the most important part of a student's engagement in the class.
- It's important for mentor teachers to model a positive attitude, even on a bad day.
- Creating a positive classroom environment and handling misbehaviors constructively will directly impact student learning.
- Being kind and empathetic when communicating with families is a great way to model positivity to new teachers.
- Teaching and modeling positive-attitude lessons with children will also help to promote this skill.

9

ADAPTABILITY AND FLEXIBILITY

- Why is adaptability important in today's classrooms?
- How can teachers model flexibility?
- What activities can be used to teach adaptability and flexibility?

IMPORTANCE OF ADAPTABILITY AND FLEXIBILITY IN TEACHING

Planning and preparing for one's classroom is a very important part of teaching. However, what happens when the day doesn't go as planned? Emergencies happen, schedules change, and events occur that make the plans change—sometimes with very little warning! Being flexible and able to adapt to the changes can help the teacher remain calm and make the day go more smoothly.

Teaching is naturally a profession that requires advance planning—partly due to administrative requirements, and partly to make sure one covers all of the necessary material for the year. Without planning, teachers would have little focus, and students would be unclear about what they are learning. However, all teachers have days that just do not go as scheduled. From an emergency drill, to a sick child, to an unannounced school assembly, teachers need to *go with the flow* and be adaptable.

Imagine teaching a beautiful lesson that took hours to plan. It is going well, and suddenly the fire alarm goes off. Of course the students' safety is of the utmost importance. Stopping everything one is doing, following the school procedures, and debriefing about safety afterwards is a requirement of the job. However, now that the flow of the lesson has been lost, students may be anxious, and the lesson is lacking fifteen minutes of teaching time. Knowing how to adapt and figure out the next steps is an important soft skill for teachers. When the plans don't go as written, teachers need to be flexible and able to adapt and change the schedule. They need to figure out which items are most important and which to omit, and what timing needs to be adjusted to fit the needs of the students. Depending on the situation, they might also need to calm the children or debrief about a drill or a school convocation if needed.

Teachers also need to address safety issues, as in the case of a severely disruptive student or an ill child. Sometimes knowing when to take an extra break to diffuse a discipline situation or call a custodian to assist in cleaning the room might need to occur. All of these events are unplanned and need to be conducted in a calm way in order to maintain order and not scare students.

Adaptability and flexibility also need to be used in cases of teaching and curriculum. Sometimes, as a teacher explains a concept, the students simply do not understand the content. Does the teacher continue to teach when the students are not comprehending? Of course not. A good teacher revamps the lesson, often at a moment's notice, to reexplain, reteach, and model in a different way.

Knowing that it is acceptable to be flexible in the teaching and draw an arrow in the lesson-plan book to continue the lesson the next day is a sign of mature decision-making and adaptability. While the content is important, if the students are not understanding it, then it's important to take a step back and figure out a better idea for the lesson. This requires adjusting both the time and the content to find a different, improved fit for the students.

Flexibility also includes adapting to school situations, such as serving on committees, working with others, and team planning. Sometimes, teachers must make changes or teach content they may not philosophically agree with. They may need to adapt to certain schedules, and work in challenging situations. All of these items will require flexibility on the part of a teacher.

ADAPTABILITY AND FLEXIBILITY

Being able to make quick decisions, think on one's feet, and adapt to new situations is a skill that is indeed important to teachers. Focusing on the challenges of flexibility and being able to make hasty decisions is a tool that all pre-service and beginning teachers need. By teaching and modeling these skills to new teachers, mentor teachers will help them to internalize these ideas and make quick but accurate decisions in their future classrooms.

The following will address how to teach and model the skills of adaptability and flexibility in classrooms.

HOW TO MODEL THESE SKILLS FOR BEGINNING TEACHERS

Beginning teachers have spent four (or more) years learning to write lesson plans and create activities for their students. They are usually comfortable with these aspects of teaching but are often not as comfortable when faced with change. Knowing how and when change is needed is a vital part of teaching, especially for those new to the profession. Here are some ways to teach the skills of adaptability and flexibility in college courses and field experiences. Flexibility is a skill that first needs to be modeled by instructors in college classes. When technology doesn't work, textbooks are on backorder, or a class schedule changes, instructors need to model flexibility and how to remain calm while still teaching the content. If students see their instructors modeling flexibility, they are more likely to apply this in their own teaching.

Adapting to change is also practiced in college courses, as state laws, professional organizations, and other stakeholders are constantly amending teacher-licensing requirements. Being able to explain these changes, make college students feel comfortable, and assist in modifying curriculum to these variations is also important at the university level.

Modeling by the mentor teacher remains important once the beginning teacher is in the classroom, whether for a field experience or student teaching. It's essential for new teachers to observe how to remain calm and composed with children when something like a fire drill occurs. Whether it's a drill or an actual event, it's important that the adult in the classroom displays this skill for the safety and well-being of the children. Hopefully, not all instances will involve emergencies. Often something as simple as a school assembly or convocation is added to the existing schedule, with little notice. It's helpful when a mentor can explain how to make appropriate decisions to deal with these unexpected schedule changes.

In some geographical areas, weather and traffic can also provide unexpected changes in schedules. A two-hour weather-related delay or a school cancellation can create a situation where change and flexibility are important. In large cities, a late bus or traffic issue can mean that several students will be late. Modeling how to make changes in the schedule or teach a lesson with only some students in attendance can be a good way to teach adaptability to new teachers.

Modeling how to be flexible is also important when working with co-workers and other colleagues. It's helpful to have a mentor teacher model this skill and come to a compromise when differences of opinion arise between co-workers. Not all teachers agree on everything, and learning to compromise by watching a mentor teacher in action is beneficial to pre-service teachers.

It's also important to allow pre-service and beginning teachers to make adaptations to lessons and other activities in the classroom. Encouraging a student teacher to develop a new seating chart, create a different incentive program, or rewrite the ending to an existing lesson will allow them to see how adaptations work while still under the watchful eye of the mentor teacher.

In summary, modeling how one deals with emergency situations and changes to curriculum and time frames is a great way to show how flexibility is used in teaching. It is also recommended that mentor teachers allow pre-service or beginning teachers to assist with these changes, or to help a new teacher to feel comfortable in doing so.

The following are some activities that can be used to teach these skills to others.

ACTIVITIES TO PRACTICE THESE SKILLS WITH NEW TEACHERS

Learning to be flexible is a skill that one doesn't learn in a textbook. It's learned when an emergency happens, a lesson does not go as planned, or a schedule is changed. It's not something that can be taught in advance, as it often requires thinking on one's feet in the middle of a lesson. Learning to be flexible happens when one has to make a different choice, teach in a varied way, or regroup when a schedule change does occur.

Some ways to practice this skill include allowing pre-service teachers to make choices and practice the skill of adaptability. Rather than assigning a *set-in-stone* type of lesson plan, instructors at the college level could allow variety and choice in planning and teaching lessons. One could assign the same concept to teach in a lesson plan but allow the class to create various lessons based on their own individual learning styles.

Flexibility could also be taught in lessons by practicing various scenarios in a pre-service classroom. Professors could provide situations in which a lesson did not go as planned, an emergency happened, or a student asked a great question that was not anticipated in the lesson. By practicing for a variety of situations, pre-service teachers will be better prepared for how to deal with them in the real world.

Another idea for practicing adaptability is to complete self-reflections after field-based lessons. These reflections could be in person with the instructor, with questions such as, "Did the lesson go exactly as planned? If not, what changed, and how did you handle this change?" These types of questions could also be in written form as guided reflections or interactive journals. Regardless of the manner in which it is completed, the idea of reflecting on the adaptations in the lesson is key.

Adaptations could also be accomplished by giving pre-service teachers or student teachers a pre-written lesson plan, such as one from a teacher's guide or textbook. Then, the student could be given situations where the lesson plan would have to be adapted to fit the needs of the students in the classroom. For example, *gearing-up* and *gearing-down* sections could be added to the lesson plan, to provide guidelines for what happens if a child already understands the material or is struggling with the concept.

Flexibility can also be taught in the student-teaching setting, or with beginning teachers. Guiding a rookie teacher through one's thought process about how to change the day when a school assembly is held or a weather delay occurs allows them to see the process in action, including how a veteran teacher cuts or diminishes the time initially allotted so that the lesson can be completed within a shorter time frame.

Being adaptable is also learned when working with others, whether they are parents, colleagues, or administrators. Sometimes others make changes that classroom teachers have no control over. Learning how to adapt to these changes in a professional manner can help beginning teachers with this skill, and will help with future dilemmas in the classroom. Unfortunately, things in the classroom do not always go as planned, and being flexible can be a great asset to new teachers.

By anticipating unplanned situations and practicing what to do when the unexpected happens, pre-service and beginning teachers will be able to see that even the best-laid plans often change. It is not due to lack of planning or poor teaching skills; it's just something that occurs in classrooms. In addition, the required curriculum may not always fit the needs of the children in the classroom. Being able to adapt and change lessons can help new teachers make the required material more suitable to the students they are teaching.

Adaptability and flexibility help new teachers with the soft skill of being able to think quickly and appropriately to make the choices they must make each day. By being prepared for the unexpected, remaining calm, and being adaptable to new situations, they will still be able to teach the curriculum and learning will still occur—maybe just not in the way they expected.

KEY IDEAS

- Emergencies happen in the classroom; teachers must be flexible in order to handle them.
- Being able to adapt curriculum is essential, as some lessons just do not go as planned.
- It's important for mentor teachers to model flexibility and adaptability in the classroom.
- Flexibility is an important skill when working with others, including colleagues and families.
- Asking a pre-service teacher for his/her ideas helps them to learn adaptability.

- Acquiring flexibility and adaptability helps new teachers learn how to *think on their feet* in the teaching profession.

10

TIME MANAGEMENT

- Why is time management important for beginning teachers?
- How can I teach and model time management?
- What are some activities to practice time management?

IMPORTANCE OF TIME MANAGEMENT IN TEACHING

Teachers are busy people. They have lessons to plan, students to teach, meetings to attend, and home lives to maintain. Teachers live by schedules and must adhere to time frames throughout their entire day. From the moment the bell rings at the beginning of the school day to the minute they pack up and leave at the end, everything seems scheduled and determined by time. As a result, teachers are forever striving to learn the soft skill of time management. They are often overheard saying things like "There's just not enough time in the day!" or "I never seem to have the time to teach everything required in the handbook." The frustration of knowing that there are only twenty-four hours in a day can complicate a teacher's life—especially for those new to the profession.

Learning the skill of time management can help even the most disorganized teacher get his/her classroom running like clockwork. Being able to figure out how to make the teaching day run in an efficient manner and effectively use the time allotted is a skill that all teachers need to learn. According to Steve Francis, author of *Time Management for Teachers*, "Time management is about control. When you allow time to control you, you never have enough of it. On the other hand, when you control your available time, you can allocate your time available to complete tasks and duties" (Francis 2018). Learning how to control and allocate time, both during and outside of the scheduled school day, is a key to success in the classroom and a major component of eliminating burnout among new teachers. As anyone in the teaching field knows, time management is an essential part of creating a successful flow to the school day. There is always somewhere to be and only a certain amount of minutes for lessons to be taught.

New teachers often learn time management the hard way—by being late to a class, having a lesson that goes well beyond the expected time frame, or not completing a required school report on time. While this method is not recommended, it definitely does teach a new teacher very quickly that time is important in schools. Time management is a skill that can be learned and developed in the classroom and is important for new teachers to acquire. In college, most students have a strict schedule to adhere to for classes, meetings, and study sessions, so part of time management is already ingrained in beginning teachers. However, applying these same skills to the classroom may require some additional effort.

It's important for everyone in a school to learn how to follow timetables, including bell schedules in junior high and high school, and lunch, recess, and special-area classes in the lower grades. Not starting classes on time, running behind schedule, or being late dropping students off to lunch impacts the students, other school workers (such as cafeteria staff), and the next class who is scheduled for lunch. Being aware and on time is not just a responsibility; it's also a courtesy to others.

Another area of time management is arriving on time, or early, to school each day. Learning to lay one's clothes out, pack one's lunch, and get materials ready the night before is always helpful to ensure timeliness. By being prepared the night before, a teacher does not have to search for the other shoe or the car keys on the way out the door in the morning. If a teacher adds a family to the list of responsibilities, this will help with parenting and getting young children prepared for day care or preschool before heading to school in the morning for his/her teaching job. Teachers who are also working parents have a great deal of responsibility on school days, and being extra prepared can really help!

Time management within the context of the school day is also important. Many new teachers struggle with the aspect of pacing during scheduled lessons, as their field experiences in college were often limited to a one-course time frame. Learning to now teach and pace for the entire day is something that takes time and experience to develop. By practicing pacing and perfecting this skill during student teaching, time management will improve as well.

In addition, time management within the entire profession of teaching is something that needs to be addressed. There is much more to teaching than simply providing lessons for eight hours a day. Planning, preparing, and grading can also take a great deal of time, and are often the parts of teaching that can be the most time-consuming. Learning to plan ahead, work collaboratively with team or subject-area teachers, and use time wisely can also impact the time management of teachers.

Determining what works best in a teacher's schedule can also be an effective way to manage time. Some teachers choose one night a week to stay late and plan for the following week, others work on Sunday afternoons, and some may arrive at school extra early in the mornings. Regardless of one's choice, learning to work around school and personal schedules is a great way to learn balance in the teaching profession.

Learning to not overcommit and knowing when to say no can also help with time management. Beginning teachers are often approached with opportunities such as club sponsorships, coaching, and committee work that can be time-consuming and invasive on one's personal life. Volunteering for just a few things and offering to help in the future is a great way for new teachers to learn balance before diving in and committing to too much.

Finally, learning to plan time for personal commitments, such as hobbies, recreational activities, or just doing something away from school is vital to a career in teaching. It's easy to spend every minute of one's day planning and grading, but self-care, including taking care of one's mental health, is also important. Teachers who learn to do this early on will be more well-balanced and are likely to stay in a teaching career longer.

In brief, time management is an important soft skill for all teachers. Beginning teachers need to practice this skill from their first day in the classroom. Being aware of time schedules during the school day, practicing the pacing of lessons, and learning to arrange for personal time are all important skills for new teachers to develop.

The next section will explain ways that mentor teachers can model this skill in their classrooms.

HOW TO MODEL THIS SKILL FOR BEGINNING TEACHERS

It is difficult for mentor teachers to model time management for pre-service and beginning teachers, simply because everyone struggles with not having enough time in the day. However, modeling this behavior for beginning teachers is an important part of preparing them for the classroom. One of the best ways that mentors can model this skill is by sharing one's own schedule and tactics for accomplishing everything one needs to do. By modeling long-term planning and sharing curriculum maps and the scope and sequence of textbooks, mentor teachers can explain the importance of both short- and long-term planning. Teachers have a great deal of material to cover in a school year, and sharing these techniques with new teachers emphasizes the significance of this skill.

Time management of the school day is also an important proficiency for mentor teachers to model. Showing pre-service teachers how to effectively manage the schedule with a concentration on pacing and transitions is key to teaching all of the lesson plans for the day without rushing or moving too slowly. This skill is only learned through experience, so allowing pre-service teachers to teach the lessons and then providing them with appropriate feedback will enable beginning teachers to improve in this area.

Another part of planning for the school day is checking to see that each part of the lesson is truly important and appropriate for the children in the classroom. Beginning teachers often tend to over-plan, or try to teach too many objectives in one lesson. Mentor teachers can help by sharing lesson plans and discussing appropriate time frames to successfully accomplish them.

Sharing personal strategies for balancing home and school is also a great way to model time management for beginning teachers. It can be eye-opening for new teachers to learn more about the need to plan, gather materials, and attend meetings. The school day contains so much more than just teaching lessons, and it's important to share this with beginners.

Mentor teachers can assist new teachers by explaining the personal parts of teaching, as well. Sharing that it's not possible to stay late on Wednesdays due to a daughter's dance lessons or a son's baseball game can benefit a new teacher by modeling how to incorporate both teaching and a family into one's schedule.

Encouraging a new teacher to manage the school day while still taking some personal time is a great discussion for mentors to have with beginning teachers. When a veteran teacher notices frustration in a new educator, reminding them that it's okay to take a night off from teaching is wonderful advice. Inviting a new teacher to dinner, taking a walk together after work, or simply sharing some relaxation techniques will help new teachers to be less stressed and more focused on time management in their future classrooms.

The following section will discuss simple strategies and activities to teach time management to pre-service and beginning teachers. Learning this skill early on will allow new teachers to make the most of their time during their teaching careers.

ACTIVITIES TO PRACTICE THIS SKILL WITH NEW TEACHERS

One of the best and most obvious ways to learn time management is simply by doing it. By allowing pre-service or practicum students to assist with planning, teach lessons within a specific time frame, and learn the schedule of the day, mentor teachers are providing the foundation for this soft skill. Also, when appropriate, allowing a student teacher to develop the plans for the entire day will prepare him/her for the real world.

Sharing a curriculum map with beginning teachers can also help to emphasize the importance of time management. While it might be nice to take an extra week or two to teach a unit, showing a map or representation of all of the lessons that need to be completed in the school term truly shows a new teacher why time management throughout the year is important.

Although it seems simple, allowing a student teacher or field experience student to take students to lunch, recess, special-area classes, and other activities is also beneficial. Taking a group of students down the hall for a restroom break can require finesse in scheduling and pacing. Emphasizing the importance of arriving at the next class on time and the impact it has on other teachers is also essential.

Sharing time management skills with children or students in upper grade levels is also a way to both model and teach the importance of scheduling, due dates, and planning ahead. Writing a schedule of the day on the board for students to see or explaining about changes in daily events will help children to adapt and plan accordingly. Children who see a well-organized teacher who is on time and respectful of others' schedules will develop this important skill in their own lives as well.

Another idea to practice time management is to share one's own plans and strategies with pre-service and beginning teachers. Sharing personal approaches—such as "I stay extra late on Thursdays to plan for the next week," or "Our grade-level team divides subject areas and plans and shares ideas so that it's more time-efficient"—can benefit beginning teachers, as they see that each schedule has to fit the individual person.

Talking about one's personal plans and recommending ways to balance work and family are also helpful ways to model this skill. Many beginning teachers are not aware of how much a teacher (especially one who has a family) has to do each week. Allowing them to see a day in a *real teacher's life* can model how important it is to balance one's valuable time between work and home. Modeling how to work around children's activities, doctor appointments, and other responsibilities is a true eye-opener for many.

Encouraging a student teacher or practicum student to attend after-school events, such as family nights, textbook adoption committee meetings, and other school-related events, also points out how much of a teacher's time is required after regular school hours. It's important to let beginning teachers know that there are many great opportunities for them to see their students in another venue as well as professional development activities in which they can participate. All of these occasions will model the necessity of good time management skills for teachers.

One final item that can help beginning teachers with their scheduling dilemmas is to recommend a teacher planning book or a calendar/agenda for writing down notes, plans, and future events. Also, in today's digital world, encouraging scheduling on cell-phone apps and lesson planning on digital formats will help tech-savvy students become well-organized teachers.

In conclusion, time management is important for a variety of reasons. It helps a beginning teacher to be better prepared, models the value of time management and meeting deadlines for children, and enables new teachers to see the importance of achieving balance in their own lives. By learning time management and perfecting it a bit more each year, teachers will be less stressed and better prepared for their daily tasks.

KEY IDEAS

- Time management is a skill that is often difficult for both beginning and veteran teachers.
- Learning to manage time is a skill that one must learn from experience. It is hard to learn from a textbook or in a class.
- Emphasizing planning, both short- and long-term, will assist a new teacher in learning time management skills.
- Knowing the skill of time management and finding a schedule that works for each individual is a valuable tool for new teachers.
- Emphasizing the idea of having a personal life away from school is key for new teachers. Helping them learn how to balance their school and home lives will help them develop as teachers.

11

ORGANIZATION

- Why is organization important for beginning teachers?
- How can I teach and model organization skills?
- What are some activities for teaching this skill to pre-service and beginning teachers?

IMPORTANCE OF ORGANIZATION SKILLS IN TEACHING

Getting organized is a vital part of the day for teachers, and having a structured and tidy classroom is of the utmost importance for success in the classroom. The soft skill of organization is one which benefits both teachers and children, and makes even a rookie teacher look proficient.

Imagine being a parent or administrator who enters a classroom which is in disarray, with no clear direction and a sense of chaos among the children. One might automatically jump to the conclusion that the teacher is disorganized and not competent in what he/she is doing. People often make quick decisions based on the appearance of the classroom—even if the teacher is very good. Now, imagine walking into a classroom where items are labeled and in their place, routines are clear and established, and children are working together in a productive way. Even if the teacher is not the best, many would assume more competence in this situation simply because of the appearance of the classroom. The old saying *First impressions are lasting* applies to classrooms as well. The first thing visitors see in a classroom is what they will remember about a teacher.

Organization skills such as being neat and tidy are important for those first impressions, but organization goes beyond just appearance. Having organization skills in the classroom will help with all areas of teaching, including instruction, management, and interactions with students. It is a soft skill that will have lasting benefits once it is learned.

Being organized implies that a teacher has planned well and is aware of the curriculum and needs of the children; the learning is structured and has meaning; and the teacher cares enough to create a safe and systematized learning environment for the classroom. Classrooms that are disorganized and in disarray may appear to be unsafe, and in fact could cause actual harm to children. Being aware of these safety issues is vital for teachers as well.

Routines and procedures are a huge part of organization. Many preservice teachers learn this skill in teacher-preparation classes, but may not be aware that procedures and routine are also helpful in organizing a classroom. Teaching students daily routines from day one will ensure that they know what to do as well as where to return items after use. The skill of teaching routines and procedures is one that demands time and effort, but is very beneficial to the overall organization of the classroom.

When routines and procedures are properly taught, the room should have a smooth flow about it. Children will know where items go without asking, teachers will be able to work with small groups without being interrupted, and substitutes will be able to proceed through the day's lessons in the absence of the regular teacher. Routines and procedures are a vital part of organization, and an important part of running a successful classroom.

Another aspect of organization is timeliness. Being aware of time and being prepared for the day is a huge part of this skill. Teachers who always know what time it is, when to transition to the next subject, and when to prepare students for events like lunch and dismissal are likely to have better classroom management and more time for teaching, and will ultimately be admired and respected by people who depend on their timely arrival.

By making sure that the class arrives to the cafeteria on time, children have more time to eat and enjoy lunch, and the cafeteria schedule does not get behind due to one late teacher. Timeliness is also appreciated by the special-area teachers (e.g., music and art classes in the elementary school) and by high school students, who won't be constantly late to their next classes. Being behind by even a few minutes impacts many others during the day.

A final part of organization includes personal organization and preparedness. Being prepared and ready for each school day—both mentally, and with materials and lesson plans in place—is also important. Teachers who are prepared will have less stress and be able to focus more on the children and their learning. Leaving the classroom in an orderly condition at the end of the day means that when one arrives the next morning, it will be ready for learning.

Being prepared and ready at home can also impact a teacher's organization. Little things like having one's clothes laid out, putting needed materials in the same place each night, and allowing enough time to get to school in the event of a traffic jam or weather issues are also parts of organization that are often not taught. A rushed teacher will probably arrive to school hurried and stressed. Being organized and ready before one even leaves the house can really help with this issue.

The skill of organization is important to every classroom, and not always easy to learn. It takes a bit of time and effort, and does not occur automatically in new teachers. The next section will explain ways that mentor teachers and college instructors can teach and model this skill.

HOW TO MODEL THIS SKILL FOR BEGINNING TEACHERS

Although modeling organization skills is easy to do, it takes initiative and forethought to teach this ability to pre-service teachers. Veteran teachers are often organized and have great routines and procedures in place; however, it's important that they remember to teach and model *how* this organization actually happens.

If one is in the classroom for field experiences, student teaching, and other practicum experiences, it's easy for beginning teachers to observe organization during the first semester of classes. Simply watching the classroom teacher explain where materials go after they are used, where to line up or sit down in the classroom, and how to do minor tasks like turning in homework can benefit a pre-service teacher simply through observation and modeling.

If one enters the classroom for these practicums in the second semester, this procedure is still doable. However, it takes some time for explanation and modeling by the classroom teacher. It's essential for pre-service teachers to ask questions like "How do the students know where to turn in homework?" or "How did you establish the rules and procedures on the first day of class?," and for mentor teachers to explain.

Although it's important to model classroom organization and the structure of things like routines and procedures, it is also vital that new teachers learn the tricks of organization as well. Little things—like placing a pencil sharpener near a trash can, or strategically placing students in seats according to their learning needs—are not always taught in a textbook, but can make or break classroom organization. Mentor teachers who think aloud and explain these little tricks to beginning teachers can help them learn organization skills for their future classrooms.

A great trick for organizing materials comes from the business world, and is called *Touch each paper only once*. As many teachers know, papers and to-do lists can accumulate; instead of allowing paperwork and memos to pile up on the desk, or in the computer in-box, teachers can model the idea of touching each paper only once. Rather than taking new papers and adding them to the pile (or saving them on a computer desktop), the teacher acts on each paper or file immediately. If a teacher receives a memo or e-mail about a school convocation, adding the date immediately to the lesson plans and then destroying or deleting the file will save a great amount of time, and prevent clutter, as well.

Another way to model organization for pre-service and beginning teachers is to ask for their input, allowing them to assist with the process. For example, a student teacher or practicum student can easily prepare the science experiment materials in advance, enabling them to learn the importance of proper organization.

Modeling organization also includes having a mentor teacher explain time factors, such as scheduling and transitions. In the upper grades, showing a new teacher how to quickly begin the next class and get students settled and ready to learn is imperative. In lower grade levels, it's helpful to model and teach how to do quick but smooth transitions from one subject to the next. The five minutes lost here and there due to poor time management and slow transitions can add up quickly in the school day, representing instruction time that cannot be regained.

ACTIVITIES TO PRACTICE THIS SKILL WITH NEW TEACHERS

Several activities can be completed in college courses and student practicums to teach the skill of organization. One of the best projects involves creating maps of future classrooms, either as grade-level teams or individuals. As the students create these maps, they should focus on all student needs, including academic, social, and safety concerns. A high school chemistry classroom, for example, would have different requirements than a kindergarten classroom. Regardless, pre-service teachers can set up a model classroom, identifying high traffic areas, student seating, and areas of need, such as where to hand in completed homework.

Another activity for beginning teachers is to allow them to deal with paperwork and forms that are needed in the classroom, as long as confidentiality issues are not concerned. Beginning teachers are often amazed by what happens *behind the scenes* in most classrooms. While this does not mean requiring student teachers to complete all of these forms alone, it does model the organization skills that they might never see otherwise.

Scheduling and time management are also important activities that can be modeled and used with beginning teachers. Often, pre-service teachers have difficulty pacing lessons and transitions between subjects or activities. Having them become more aware of time can help them improve this skill—for example, using a stopwatch app on a cell phone to help them learn how to move swiftly but efficiently through a lesson while still covering the required content.

Along with lesson planning and pacing, another important skill to teach is that of long-term planning for the semester, or even the school year. Students in college courses often focus on only one lesson, or possibly a unit at a time, and are often not aware of the long-term strategies that teachers must employ in their classrooms. Modeling and creating curriculum maps and learning how to plan for the entire school year is another essential skill for today's teachers.

Self-organization can also be taught in college courses. Teaching mini lessons about the importance of being prepared for the day, including setting out your clothing the night before and having materials ready in advance, can have a positive impact on the school day and help the students be successful both in student teaching and in their own future classrooms.

Commenting on great organization when one observes it can also benefit future teachers. People often demonstrate organizational skills unconsciously; being organized is seen as automatic, or often only noticed in its absence. Praising students when they are especially prepared for lessons—by having their materials ready, timers in place, and roles and responsibilities written in advance—can underscore the importance of this essential skill.

Many veteran teachers say that they are just not organized, or that if they ever put things away in their proper places, they would never be able to find them. However, as one examines the careful organization of others and discovers ways to teach these same skills to children, new teachers will discover that they have created a well-run, finely organized classroom.

By learning the skill of organization, pre-service teachers will acquire the ideas needed to manage children, materials, and time. Being organized shows that they care about the classroom in which they teach as well as the children they are teaching. An organized educator will be able to teach lessons, provide a safe learning environment, and look like a professional, even in their first days in the classroom.

KEY IDEAS

- Organization is important, as it implies a professional and orderly classroom.
- An organized teacher also models this skill for his/her students.
- Scheduling and time management are a vital part of organization for teachers.
- Routines and procedures are crucial to the organization of the classroom, regardless of grade level.

- Modeling organization for pre-service and beginning teachers is an important part of preparing future educators.
- Organization is vital for the safety and well-being of students.

12

INITIATIVE

- Why is initiative important to beginning teachers?
- How can I model this skill for pre-service and beginning teachers?
- What are some activities that can be used to practice this skill?

IMPORTANCE OF INITIATIVE IN TEACHING

According to Business Dictionary.com, the word *initiative* means "An individual's action that begins a process, often done without direct managerial influence" (Business Dictionary 2018). Although this soft skill is often assessed in the business world, it certainly applies to education as well. Teachers who show initiative *go above and beyond* the normal expectations of teachers, and often do so without being asked.

Teachers who show initiative are those still at school after the bell rings, the ones who volunteer for extra projects and see issues that need to be addressed. They are often proactive and work to prevent problems rather than dealing with them after they happen. They stop to pick up that piece of trash on the floor or help a child who is not assigned to them. They believe in the African proverb *It takes a village to raise a child*, as they are ready to step in and help *any* child in the school, not just the ones on their class lists.

Teachers with initiative volunteer for the extra tasks in a school day, from sponsoring a club to piloting a new reading program to attending extra professional development in the summer. They never ask if they will be compensated for the extra work. Instead, they do it happily, with little reward or notice from others. They do it because it's the right thing to do.

In the classroom, a teacher shows initiative by going above and beyond the expectations of teaching. He/she provides additional assistance for struggling students, differentiates instruction to meet the needs of every student, and notices when a child does not feel well, or is behaving differently than normal. He/she is not afraid to seek out resources or find assistance for those who need support. No one has to ask someone with strong initiative for help; he/she just offers it.

Initiative is the soft skill that determines the difference between a proficient student teacher and a distinguished one. Initiative is not just doing the minimum in college classes but going above and beyond the course expectations. It is helping a partner with a class project and doing more than what is expected in class discussions and other assignments.

By learning and practicing initiative at the college level, pre-service teachers will be able to take this skill with them into the teaching profession. Reference letters indicating that a student has shown extra initiative will catch the eye of potential employers, as this soft skill is always in demand.

Administrators also look for initiative when they conduct teacher evaluations and job performance reviews. A teacher who goes the extra mile and is not afraid to do a little more—serve on a committee, help a student who just needs some extra time—is always noticed by a principal.

Initiative in a school setting also means offering to help in ways that go beyond a school day. Volunteering to pilot a new program, attending extra in-service training after school, or offering to work on a new problem shows individual initiative and is also appreciated by school administrators. They recognize the added efforts of a teacher and know who in the building is willing to go the extra mile.

Another example of initiative in teachers is being proactive rather than reactive. Teachers who demonstrate initiative see problems in the building and try to determine ways to help. They don't wait for solutions to happen. Instead, they seek to solve problems and find answers to recurring difficulties. Teachers with initiative help students solve their own problems and are always looking for new ideas and solutions.

Students also know which teachers show initiative in their teaching. They are the teachers who stay after school to coach sports, sponsor clubs, and help tutor students during their lunch periods. They are often the ones that students reach out to when they have a problem, because they know they can count on these teachers to find a solution.

Modeling initiative for student teachers will help them see the power of hard work and provide an incentive for students to do this as well. The next section will explain some ways that college professors and classroom teachers can model this skill for future teachers.

HOW TO MODEL THIS SKILL FOR BEGINNING TEACHERS

It takes inspiration and planning on the part of college instructors and classroom teachers to model the soft skill of initiative. Many college professors show extra initiative in their jobs, but sometimes students are not aware of this when they attend class. Being able to explain that the job does not end at the completion of class but takes extra time and effort—to finish grading student assignments, serve on committees, and carry out additional research and planning—can make an impact on future teachers.

Mentor teachers can also do the same thing in elementary and secondary classrooms. Again, while many people show initiative, they often don't receive accolades for doing so. Telling pre-service teachers about the extra efforts and activities that come along with a teaching career can model this skill.

Inviting pre-service and beginning teachers to participate in committees, extracurricular activities, and other school projects will enable them to not only witness the initiative shown by veteran teachers but also allow them to develop this skill as well. As long as a beginning teacher does not try to volunteer for every school committee or take on more than one can possibly do, this is a great skill to encourage in those new to the profession.

On that note, mentor teachers also need to explain the importance of maintaining a balance between classroom responsibilities and taking on extra projects for the school. While it looks great to administrators when new teachers volunteer for everything, it is also important to teach them that it's even better to *do one thing and do it well*. Reminding rookie teachers that they should be involved but in a reasonable, doable way is an important part of modeling initiative.

Initiative also involves taking the lead on projects and involving others in the work. Successful teachers can show initiative by taking the lead, but they are also careful to involve others so that the impact of new ideas can be even more powerful. By sharing the workload and involving other teachers and faculty members, the teacher can show initiative while allowing others to share the credit.

Teachers who show initiative don't do it for rewards or accolades; they simply do it because it's the right thing to do, and because it will benefit children in the end. Good teachers do more than what's required, often putting in hours of unpaid time because they know it will help educate the children in their classrooms. Initiative is appreciated by others, and it can also help one's own self-esteem in the process. By helping others, and doing more than what's required, new teachers feel good about themselves and the work they are doing.

The following section includes some ways to practice initiative. By practicing this skill before entering the teaching profession, pre-service teachers are apt to be better educators and learn ways to show initiative before entering the classroom.

ACTIVITIES TO PRACTICE THIS SKILL WITH NEW TEACHERS

Initiative among beginning teachers is often already ingrained in them. Parents teach the skill of initiative from a very early age, encouraging their children to do the right thing, volunteer to help others, and go above and beyond in school projects and extracurricular areas. Many pre-service teachers arrive at college or practicum experiences with this skill already in place, but what happens to those who don't have initiative when they arrive in classrooms?

Teaching and practicing initiative is a skill that is most often taught through modeling. Encouraging a pre-service teacher to get involved with school activities is a great way to start. Providing opportunities for practicum and student teachers to become immersed in the school environment helps to develop their teaching skills and work ethic and also shows them that teachers have tasks that extend beyond the school day. Many such opportunities exist, including volunteering for a family event or helping with an afterschool activity, that are not terribly time-consuming and can be completed during a college course or student teaching. College professors or mentor teachers can help teach initiative by encouraging pre-service teachers to participate in these events and then discussing them afterwards.

Noticing when a pre-service or student teacher exhibits initiative is a helpful way to encourage this trait in future teachers. Simply saying "Thank you" to a student teacher who grades an extra stack of papers, or works ahead in the planning, can go a long way. Since initiative often goes unnoticed, finding ways to recognize it in a beginning teacher can reinforce this valuable attribute.

Connecting a new teacher to others in the school who practice great initiative is also a great way to strengthen this skill. In every school there are certain people who are enthusiastic about their job and encourage others to become involved and active in the school community. Making sure that new teachers in the school are introduced and connected to these people will help provide role models and mentors for those new to the profession.

Providing opportunities for pre-service and beginning teachers to help problem-solve is another strategy for teaching and modeling initiative. Allowing a pre-service teacher to participate in grade-level or subject-area planning meetings can be a great way to involve them in the school environment while encouraging them to help with planning and problem-solving. Often beginning teachers have fresh ideas that can help a team with a new project or technique, and they will feel appreciated for doing so.

Working with a school-based team on a problem-solving activity also helps in the area of practicing initiative with beginning teachers. Even attending one Response to Intervention (RTI) meeting or a team planning event can help a beginning teacher learn how to be a team player and help solve problems. By seeing such strategies modeled by veteran teachers, a new teacher will be more likely to follow this example in their own teaching career.

Overall, the soft skill of initiative means showing a willingness to work hard, to go above and beyond the expectations of a teaching job, and to do these activities without being asked. Initiative is the skill that will set beginning teachers apart from others. It shows that a teacher is a problem-solver, a risk-taker, and someone who genuinely cares about the teaching profession. Initiative in the field of education is important, as it provides the power to create teachers who help children, find new ways to solve problems in the classroom, and discover innovative strategies for school improvement. While teachers may not be directly compensated or rewarded for their initiative, it is a skill that administrators notice and students appreciate.

By learning the soft skill of initiative at an early stage in their careers, beginning teachers will see the importance of this disposition in education, and in other areas of their lives as well. Initiative is needed in anything one does in life and goes far beyond the walls of the classroom.

KEY IDEAS

- Initiative is the idea of going above and beyond the requirements in teaching.
- Teachers who show initiative volunteer for committees, complete extra training, and do more than the minimum in their jobs.
- Showing initiative in the area of problem-solving can help both the students and the school in which one teaches.
- Showing initiative during student teaching can mean the difference between becoming a proficient, or a distinguished, student teacher.
- Practicing the soft skill of initiative is noted on teaching evaluations and appreciated by administrators.
- Modeling initiative benefits both pre-service teachers and students alike, as it shows that a teacher is not afraid of hard work.

13

PROFESSIONALISM

- Why is professionalism important for beginning teachers?
- How can I teach and model professionalism skills?
- What are some activities for teaching this skill to pre-service and beginning teachers?

IMPORTANCE OF PROFESSIONALISM IN TEACHING

Professionalism is a soft skill that is vital to both getting a teaching job and keeping one. One of the first characteristics judged at a teaching job interview is the idea of professionalism. Was the applicant on time? Was he/she dressed professionally and appropriately? Did the applicant use good manners and look the interviewer in the eye while speaking? Since first impressions are lasting, it is important to practice professionalism from the first minute one walks into an interview. Knowing how to interview and practice professionalism is a skill that all new teachers need and should be taught at the college level in teacher-preparation courses. Learning about resources at the university, such as career and job placement services, is also vital to acquiring the soft skill of professionalism, and will help beginning teachers secure jobs.

After securing a teaching position, professionalism is a skill that will be assessed in teachers for the rest of their careers. Being a teacher means that others are always watching your actions—both in- and outside of school. Watching one's actions and acting in a professional manner are important both in the classroom and on weekends, when out with friends. Being aware that students (or their parents) could be watching reminds teachers to always act in a professional way.

Professionalism in the classroom includes many components, from the way one treats the children, to how one works with others, to how one reacts to suggestions and constructive criticism. It's important to remember to act professionally with others—even those one may not agree with—at all times. Behaving in a respectful and kind manner to everyone is a major part of professionalism in the teaching world.

Accepting advice and listening to suggestions are other key parts of professionalism in teaching. If a supervisor or administrator provides suggestions for improvement or mentions that certain strategies need to be strengthened, it is essential for both student teachers and beginning teachers to openly listen to the suggestions and attempt to fix those areas. Showing that one is prepared to accept criticism and modify old ideas implies that the teacher is a willing learner and an adaptable person.

Using and modeling appropriate language skills, both written and spoken, is also considered an integral part of professional behavior. Remembering that one is modeling appropriate grammar to students while teaching, and showing appropriate written mechanics in letters and notes to parents, models that a teacher cares enough to be professional in everything he/she does. The proper use of electronic media is also an important part of professional behavior. In addition to the social media aspects that were mentioned in an earlier chapter, remembering to return texts and e-mails in a timely manner and practicing a professional tone are also key skills for beginning teachers.

Another part of professionalism includes dressing professionally while in the classroom. Although many schools have adopted a more casual dress style, student teachers and beginning teachers should remember that these first experiences are considered a *continuous job interview*. Since most teaching contracts are provisional or probationary at the beginning of the term, looking just a bit more professional and *dressing for success* can make a difference to many administrators. Also, students who see their teachers dressed professionally are apt to treat them in a more respectful way. They are more likely to show proper behavior and treat the information and teaching provided as important. In fact, some principals insist that teachers *dress up* and look even more professional during high-stakes testing. Simply modeling that the work of taking tests is important can help students apply this same attitude in their own learning.

Other aspects of professionalism include being on time, completing tasks on schedule, and generally following the rules and expectations of the school. If teachers expect children to arrive in class on time and ready to learn, then teachers need to be on time (or early), and ready to teach. If the school policy is that homework is to be completed on time, then teachers need to be on time with handing in paperwork and returning graded items.

In addition, although most school rules are written with the children in mind, they certainly apply to adults in the building as well. If children are not allowed to chew gum during class, then teachers should not chew gum. If the children are supposed to abide by a certain dress code, the teacher needs to obey this as well. It is important for teachers to be aware of the school rules and policies. Following the same rules as the children models respect for the school as well as the importance of such policies.

The soft skill of being professional is one that will be measured and evaluated from the beginning of one's teaching career until the day one retires. Being aware of how one treats others, acting responsibly with timeliness and due dates, and being respectful of school rules and policies are all ways in which professionalism is measured.

The following section provides ways to model and teach professionalism in university classes and future classrooms.

HOW TO MODEL THIS SKILL FOR BEGINNING TEACHERS

University professors and classroom mentors are some of the first to model professionalism for pre-service teachers. From the time students begin college in search of an education degree, they watch the teachers and professors in their classrooms. From their first day of classes, college students witness their professors modeling respect for others, using proper teaching techniques, and upholding personal characteristics, such as punctuality. Seeing individuals who are kind and respectful and acting in a professional way is a powerful testament to the importance of professionalism in the field of teaching.

Modeling how to work with others is another aspect of professionalism. Although teachers may not always agree with the people they work with, it's important to always be kind and to show respect. Veteran teachers who avoid cliques and negative behaviors toward others can model this very important behavior for beginning teachers. Also, noting that *all* employees in a school are important and showing them respect is part of the soft skill of professionalism. Remembering to thank the custodian for vacuuming the classroom, appreciating the secretary for doing his/her job, and showing kindness and respect to paraprofessionals are important ways mentor teachers can reinforce this skill. Remembering that everyone in the school is there for the same mission of educating children, regardless of their educational background, can be a huge lesson for beginning teachers.

It is also important to show new teachers how to act with parents and families. In elementary grades, modeling respect to parents and allowing them to discuss concerns in parent–teacher conferences is important, while in the upper grades, modeling how to make a parent phone call about an uncomfortable situation will help as well. Mentor teachers can help a new teacher remember that parents are the true experts in their child's lives, and it's essential to always treat them with respect.

Following school rules and procedures is also imperative. Though a veteran teacher may be tempted to not follow the rules or make unprofessional choices, it is important to remind student teachers and beginning mentees about these policies, as they can determine whether or not a new teacher retains his or her position.

Being timely and keeping deadlines is another key area to demonstrate to student teachers and others beginning in the teaching profession. If a report is due to the principal by a certain date, making sure it is on time (or early) is a crucial skill for a new teacher to learn. If the students are to be at a special-area class or change high school classes at a certain time, acknowledging this and being respectful of others' time is important.

Modeling composure, even on a bad day, is another essential skill for mentors and instructors. Everyone has a bad day on occasion, but what one does about it can make a difference to a beginning teacher. When parents become angry, students behave badly, or the paperwork stacks up, it's important to know how to maintain one's composure. When a mentor teacher has a rough day, discussing it with pre-service teachers provides a great opportunity for him or her to explain how they handled the situation. While teachers are human, it is imperative to remain calm and composed at all times. Discussing ways the mentor teacher was able to *keep her cool* during these situations will help new teachers when they have to deal with difficult experiences of their own.

The next section will provide suggestions and activities for practicing the skill of professionalism both in the classroom and in other situations.

ACTIVITIES TO PRACTICE THIS SKILL WITH NEW TEACHERS

Teaching professionalism and competence can benefit everyone in the classroom, even children. A teacher who uses good manners will likely create students who use good manners. Noticing and praising children when they make proper decisions can go a long way in today's world. By creating an environment of kindness and good manners, a beginning teacher will be more likely to exhibit this behavior as well.

It's also helpful to show beginning teachers how to work well with others and participate in co-teaching situations. With inclusion practices and paraprofessionals in many classrooms, modeling respect for others and working together to teach the students is another important aspect of professionalism. It also models to students how to work together kindly and proficiently in their own group work.

Modeling respect for parents and families is also an important part of professionalism, regardless of differences in background or education. It's important to model caring, patience, and a willingness to listen. Knowing that parents were the child's *first teachers* can provide meaningful explanations about the child's habits and learning styles, and asking for this information implies a level of professionalism and respect in the classroom.

Attributes such as being on time, completing reports before deadlines, and following directions may seem obvious, but these are important as well. These professional characteristics are often some of the first items noted in beginning teachers, and the lack of these skills can even be a cause for disciplinary issues, or dismissal.

Admitting one's mistakes and asking for help are also keys to professionalism. Beginning teachers are not expected to know everything about the curriculum, school procedures, and the administration. However, administrators notice if a new teacher admits that he/she made a mistake and asks for help and advice; it makes it far more likely that they will view the new teacher as professional, and a willing learner.

Dressing and acting professionally is another part of this soft skill. While it is important to dress comfortably in the classroom, dressing a notch above the students will model that the teacher is in charge, and a professional. Also, dressing appropriately for events such as Meet the Teacher Night and Open House is important, as this is often where new teachers make their first impression on parents and families.

Acting professionally with children and students also accompanies this soft skill. One of the most common errors beginning teachers make is forgetting that they need to *be friendly without being a friend*. A teacher is an instructor in the classroom and a role model to the students. Acting like an adult and not a student is important here. Of course, educators should have fun and enjoy teaching, but remembering to be mature and in charge is key to the skill of professionalism. If students know the limits in the classroom and see the teacher acting in a professional manner, they are less likely to misbehave.

Many pre-service teachers are evaluated on dispositions and personal characteristics. Applying the practice of teaching and evaluating professionalism should be reflected in a course syllabus and in classroom observations at the college level. Dispositions that are addressed in teacher-preparation institutions often center around the ideas of professionalism and expertise in the classroom. These same concepts will most likely be evaluated in a similar manner in one's future teaching position.

Knowing how to interview in a professional manner and to practice professionalism in the classroom is a skill that all new teachers need and should be taught at the university level in teacher-preparation courses. Participating in mock interviews in college courses or through career services at the university will help to prepare beginning teachers for these experiences. Interviewing is often a cause of anxiety for new teachers, and practicing the professional skills associated with it can be very helpful.

In general, the keys to professionalism are learning this soft skill in college courses, having a mentor who models and teaches appropriate educator behaviors, and being able to practice these skills during practicums and student teaching. Being held accountable for professional behaviors *before* one enters the classroom for the first time is important for teachers as well as the students they will one day instruct.

KEY IDEAS

- Professionalism is necessary from the interview process to the last day of one's career.
- Professionalism includes the way a teacher treats students, parents, and others with whom he/she works.
- Beginning teachers also need to learn how to communicate in a professional way.
- Being professional embraces many ideas, including being on time, following due dates, accepting criticism, and being willing to admit mistakes and seek advice.
- Professionalism is noticed by others and can be a reason for job termination. It is crucial to remediate the lack of professional skills in teachers if needed.
- Teachers should practice professionalism beginning in their pre-service classrooms, and throughout their entire teaching careers.

14

WORK ETHIC

- Why is a good work ethic important to beginning teachers?
- How can I model this skill for pre-service and beginning teachers?
- What are some activities that can be used to practice this skill?

IMPORTANCE OF A GOOD WORK ETHIC IN TEACHING

According to *Merriam-Webster's Dictionary*, a work ethic is defined as "a set of values centered on the importance of doing work and reflected especially in a desire or determination to work hard" (Merriam-Webster 2018). Having a good work ethic is valuable in today's classrooms. Teachers need to want to do their best and be willing to work hard. They need to model this soft skill to their students, as instilling a good work ethic in children is the ultimate goal of teaching.

A proper work ethic is also important to parents. Parents want their children's teachers to be good people who have a desire to work hard at the job of educating their students. They want their children to be in the care of well-rounded, ambitious, and caring adults. Parents want to know that when they put their children on the bus each morning, they will be greeted by teachers who have a passion for their job and will do their very best to educate them.

A good work ethic involves going above and beyond the minimum expectations. In teaching, it means doing additional work to help a child learn a new skill. It means working extra time in the evenings to prepare for the next day and giving up part of their summer to attend classes and professional development activities. It means volunteering to help with the elementary school carnival or the high school dance, without wondering if one will be compensated for it. It means spending lunch hour in one's classroom to listen to a student who is having trouble at home or school. A good work ethic means doing the right thing and keeping the needs of students foremost in one's planning and teaching.

A good work ethic also involves being a moral person with good values. Children often learn simple behaviors such as honesty and good manners from watching the adults in their lives. It's important for new teachers to have these values and principles. Integrity—the idea of doing the right thing even when no one is watching—is a valuable part of a good work ethic. Teachers are held to higher standards than other professionals because they have a direct impact on children, and integrity is an important part of this.

Making good decisions in the classroom and in one's personal life is also part of a good work ethic. Being professional, on time, appropriately dressed, and ready for teaching are all important decisions that an educator needs to make. Being aware of one's behavior in public is valuable as well. Parents and administrators are watching and will take note of poor behavior, even if it takes place outside of school.

It's also important to be careful with social media and other aspects of one's personal life. It is imperative to ensure that anything posted for public view is ethical and tasteful, as it reveals the values and ethics of the person making the posts. Parents and administrators viewing photos that are not appropriate could lead to them seeing the teacher in a different—and possibly negative—light.

Another aspect of a good work ethic includes admitting one's mistakes. All beginning teachers make mistakes; being able to admit them to a fellow teacher or administrator is part of a notable work ethic. Instead of hiding mistakes or lying about them, new teachers need to admit them and seek advice for how to better handle such issues in the future. A caring administrator knows that mistakes happen and can assist the new teacher in remediating them in an empathetic way.

An admirable work ethic in the teaching profession includes all aspects of professionalism and is a soft skill that can make or break a new teacher's career. Using good judgment, making moral decisions, and doing what's right are all aspects of this skill along with working hard and doing one's absolute best for the children in one's classroom.

The value of a good work ethic starts at a very young age, and by exhibiting this skill for students in the classroom, the teacher can become a role model as well. Simultaneously learning and teaching this skill can be an interesting experience for beginning teachers and can lead to many positive things in the classroom and in all future endeavors.

The following will provide ways that professors and mentor teachers can model this skill for pre-service and beginning teachers.

HOW TO MODEL THIS SKILL FOR BEGINNING TEACHERS

It goes without saying that college instructors and mentor teachers are crucial when it comes to modeling a good work ethic for future teachers. The way that "teachers of teachers" behave and model professionalism helps to build the foundation for how new educators will develop this skill. If a mentor teacher arrives late to school every day, complains about the job, and treats others in an unkind way, a new teacher may develop these characteristics as well. However, if a mentor models professional skills, a positive mind-set, and respect for others, the new teacher will notice and hopefully follow suit.

By modeling professional skills such as timeliness, respect for others, and honesty, an instructor or mentor teacher is teaching these skills to new teachers, often without realizing it. How a mentor teacher handles a difficult situation and treats others in the building can have a huge impact on the attitude of new teachers assigned to him or her. Teachers deal with difficult situations on a daily basis, whether it's handling a behavior issue or working with upset parents. It is easy to *lose one's cool*, become upset, and say the wrong thing. However, remembering to model professional behavior, and look for the positive, can teach a beginning teacher how to handle these issues in his/her future classroom.

It's also important for mentor teachers to model respect for others. Remembering to be kind to *all* employees in the building is important, as one interacts with paraprofessionals, custodians, cafeteria workers, and administrative assistants. Treating all people with respect and kindness is also part of modeling a good work ethic for new teachers.

Going above and beyond in the classroom and volunteering to help with school events, a special project, and other items in a school setting are also great ways to model a good work ethic. These actions show that a teacher cares and wants to do a good job in their profession. Inviting a practicum student or student teacher to assist in these projects can set the tone for this level of hard work in their future classroom.

Sharing ideas with beginning teachers about being professional, working hard, and showing extra initiative are valuable tools for a mentor teacher to use when modeling a good work ethic. Building self-esteem in new teachers and offering to help and listen to their concerns can teach the importance of helping others become education professionals.

The media and the outside world often make unkind comments about teaching and education in general. Reassuring new teachers that their work and perseverance are indeed valued and respected is a way to help them see themselves as professionals, and will help them to develop a positive work ethic even in the midst of unkind words.

Overall, one of the most important things a mentor teacher can do for a beginning teacher is to model the traits of a professional work ethic. Following school procedures, assisting with projects that show extra initiative, and doing what's right in front of new teachers means that one is modeling appropriate skills for the teachers with whom they will work in the future.

A professional work ethic is not something new teachers learn by reading a textbook; it's something they learn by watching others. By being an appropriate role model, explaining one's behaviors and choices, and discussing the importance of this skill with new teachers, a mentor teacher can have a huge impact on new teachers. Here are some ways to teach a good work ethic in the classroom.

ACTIVITIES TO PRACTICE THIS SKILL WITH NEW TEACHERS

There are many activities one can use to teach a good work ethic. Although the modeling techniques mentioned above are probably the most important, there are many other activities a beginning teacher can do to practice this soft skill in the classroom.

First, taking the time to explain school expectations, classroom procedures, and other information to pre-service and beginning teachers is important. Because every school has its own unique needs, explaining these areas to a new teacher is imperative. A new teacher orientation, student teaching handbook, or a quick meeting to explain school procedures will help teach a good work ethic. It is hard to know how to behave unless expectations are clearly stated and explained for beginning teachers.

Having an entire staff that is open and available to help and encourage new teachers is also essential in promoting a good work ethic in beginning teachers. It's reassuring to see the teacher across the hall model kindness, share information and materials, and notice the hard work and efforts of a beginning teacher. If someone encourages the strength and determination of a new teacher, the impact will be lasting and will instill the idea that a good work ethic is not only important for the teacher, but also appreciated by others.

Encouraging new teachers to participate in an extracurricular activity, school event, or something outside of the school day is also an excellent way to teach a positive work ethic. Sometimes new teachers want to help and simply need an invitation or extra nudge to feel welcome and needed. Showing this extra initiative is part of establishing a good work ethic and can be a determining factor in keeping one's teaching job for many years to come.

A mentor teacher or administrator may uncover some areas of concern when working with new teachers, such as when they are late arriving to school, don't complete required school reports, or don't appear to give 100 percent in the classroom. Knowing when to intervene and have heart-to-heart conversations with beginning teachers about the value of maintaining these professional behaviors is an important part of mentoring them.

Having difficult conversations with pre-service and new teachers about professionalism, a poor work ethic, and other concerns is not easy. However, when veteran educators point out the errors in a kind and helpful way, they can assist new teachers in learning strategies to remediate them and be successful in these areas in the future. By offering ways to help, providing encouragement, and even sharing stories about one's own past blunders, new teachers will learn that mistakes happen, but can be a learning experience on the road toward becoming a professional. Providing feedback—whether informally, or on required written evaluations—is one of the best ways to help a struggling teacher with professional and ethical issues they simply may not have been taught in education classes or from life experiences.

Overall, the value of a good work ethic is extremely important for beginning teachers, because what they learn in their first years of teaching will follow them throughout their entire careers. A positive work ethic can mean the difference between keeping one's job and being dismissed for poor job performance. Learning this vital skill through the guidance of mentor teachers and school administrators will help new teachers start their profession on a solid footing.

KEY IDEAS

- A good work ethic means that a teacher works hard, does the right thing, and has positive values.
- A good work ethic includes having an affirming attitude, being respectful to others, and making the right choices during the school day, and beyond.
- A good work ethic includes going above and beyond the required responsibilities of a classroom teacher.
- A work ethic is not just about what one teaches but how one acts and presents oneself in the classroom.
- Discussing and remediating characteristics of a poor work ethic is an important priority for a mentor teacher or administrator.
- Learning a good work ethic in the first years of teaching will help new educators throughout their entire teaching careers.

CONCLUSION

- Why does all of this matter to new teachers?
- How are soft skills important to veteran teachers and those who mentor new teachers?
- What are the next steps to increasing soft skills in the teaching profession?

SOFT SKILLS AND NEW TEACHERS

Many college professors and school administrators will claim that new teachers are lacking in soft skills, such as communication, teamwork, and professionalism in the workplace. There are multiple theories as to why soft skills are lacking in new teachers, including a failure to teach them in K–12 schools and in higher education. There is also a belief that new teachers have a sense of entitlement, or a feeling that they deserve jobs simply because they have gone to college and completed the required teaching curriculum. This is often associated with the Millennial generation, those born in the 1980s and 1990s. Although not all new teachers are Millennials, a large majority of them are, and this sense of entitlement could be a contributing factor.

Another possible theory for why beginning teachers are lacking in soft skills has to do with the increase in technology. According to Howell (2017), "The younger generation's strength is partly to blame for its weakness. Because Millennials are so proficient and reliant on technology, many of them haven't properly developed other skills apart from working on digital devices." Because technology is so prevalent in today's world, many younger teachers have grown up with proficiencies such as texting and e-mailing but may be lacking in soft skills, such as face-to-face communication. Although the use of technology will be useful to future teachers as a hard skill, it may be one reason why many of today's beginning teachers lack some of these soft skills.

Regardless of why new professionals are often deficient in soft skills, the good news is that these skills are teachable and able to be remediated. This book offers a discussion on how to develop these skills in the teaching profession. The preceding chapters examine the definition of each soft skill and how they relate to teaching as well as ways to model and teach them to beginning educators. These soft skills are important in education and are valued by students, parents, and administrators. They are also vital to getting and keeping jobs in the teaching profession. In a recent article in *Forbes* magazine, Lisa Rabasca Roepe stated that "Failing to show soft skills at a job interview can cost you the job. According to the report, 75% of recruiting professionals have cut an interview short because a candidate didn't demonstrate the soft skills needed for the position they had applied for" (Roepe 2017).

By having the soft skills outlined in this book, those who work with future educators in college preparation, field experiences, and the first years of teaching will have some valuable tools to help them be successful. These skills are all important in teaching and are also important to model for the students in one's future classroom.

Communication skills are vital in teaching new content to children and in communicating with parents, colleagues, and administrators. More teachers today communicate through technology and social media, so it's even more important to learn how to share new ideas effectively, talk respectfully to parents about concerns, and work well with others in a school setting.

Confidence, or believing in oneself, is valuable, because it sets the tone for the classroom. Teachers who look confident and self-assured are more likely to teach without hesitation, feel more in control, and have better classroom management. Students can tell when a teacher is lacking confidence, so being able to portray this soft skill in the classroom is a must for new teachers.

Enthusiasm makes a classroom joyful, pleasant, and fun to participate in, both for the teacher and the students. Educators who exhibit enthusiasm can make lessons more exciting, thus making students more motivated, and allowing teachers to enjoy doing their jobs. By showing enthusiasm for teaching, a future educator can portray passion and interest, extremely beneficial for teachers and students alike.

Creativity also makes a classroom more fun; when teachers are creative, their students are more interested and excited about lessons. Creative teachers enhance curiosity, motivation, and a love of learning in the classroom. Teachers who think outside the box and use new strategies and techniques can help students gain a love of learning simply by being passionate about what they teach.

Decision-making skills help beginning teachers solve problems, make wise choices, and be better prepared for life in the classroom. Because they make so many decisions during the school day, learning to be competent in this area is an important soft skill for beginning teachers. By practicing decision-making in pre-service education classes, new teachers will be better prepared to use this skill in the classroom.

Teamwork and collaboration are increasingly used in today's classrooms. As more schools employ grade-level and subject-area teams, it's even more important for new teachers to be able to collaborate and work well with others. Learning this skill in college courses and practicums will assist new teachers in future team experiences.

Stress management is a soft skill that every teacher needs. Teaching can be a stressful job. There are lessons to plan, parents to communicate with, and students to manage. Being able to handle stress and learn coping skills will help new teachers deal with difficult situations in teaching. It's also important to learn how to focus on self-care and ensure that one has time away from the classroom.

A *positive attitude* can make or break one's time in the teaching profession. Coming to school with a great attitude and remaining positive will impact not only how the teacher performs but how the students perform as well. Being constructive and encouraging to students creates a classroom environment where students love learning and the teacher loves teaching.

Adaptability and flexibility are important to teachers as well. Even though teachers have lesson plans and are prepared for the day, schedules change and lessons are disrupted. Being able to go with the flow while remaining calm is an important soft skill for new teachers. Preparing for changes and interruptions during the day is a skill that one can never practice enough.

Time management goes along with flexibility. Being prepared and using one's time wisely is an important skill for teachers. Learning to pace lessons, use proper transitions, and follow timelines is vital to ensure a smooth flow in the classroom and will help new teachers make the most of their school day.

Organization is vital to a classroom as well. Teachers who are organized know where materials are located, have spaces for the children to learn, and are well prepared for teaching. Being able to organize a classroom and everything in it is essential for all educators but especially important for beginning teachers.

Initiative means going above and beyond the call of duty in the classroom. Teachers who show initiative do things without being asked, volunteer for activities outside the classroom, and are proactive when it comes to solving problems. Initiative is noticed by administrators and a great skill to develop in the first years of teaching.

Professionalism includes everything from the way a teacher acts to how he/she dresses or speaks with others. It includes being on time, dressing appropriately, and being the adult in the classroom. Professionalism also includes how one acts outside the school, one of the responsibilities associated with being an educator.

A *work ethic* is how one performs the job of teaching. It includes being able to work hard, be positive, and have a moral commitment to the field of education. Teachers who have a good work ethic greatly contribute to the overall excellence and culture of the school.

While this book only identifies fourteen soft skills that future educators need to possess in order to be successful, there are many more that impact both the teaching and the learning that occurs in a classroom. However, by starting with the fourteen that are outlined in this book, beginning teachers will have an idea of the range of skills they need to acquire, and mentor teachers will know which skills to model and practice when they are supervising new teachers.

CONCLUSION

SOFT SKILLS AND VETERAN TEACHERS

Although this book is directed toward beginning teachers, it's equally important for veteran teachers to embrace these soft skills, since they are the mentors and role models that new teachers look up to and observe on a daily basis. These skills are important for *any* teacher, and being reminded of these qualities can help a veteran teacher as well. According to a recent report from the Department of Labor, "Interestingly, research also suggests that soft skills are not just important for first-time employees. According to a poll released in June 2008 by the Society for Human Resource Management (SHRM), many workplace soft skills have become more important for the experienced professional" (US Department of Labor 2012). Veteran teachers can sometimes use a reminder that soft skills can help anyone in the teaching profession.

In addition, many veteran teachers want to *give back to the profession*. Teaching other teachers and inducting them into the field of education is not only an honor but a duty of practicing educators everywhere. By welcoming new teachers into their classrooms and nurturing their skills, veteran teachers can help in many ways. Through modeling and instructing, experienced teachers not only help beginning teachers but can also refine and improve their own skills as well. Inviting new teachers into one's classroom can be intimidating, but by doing so, veteran teachers can model, represent, and teach those skills that are vital to the success of beginning teachers.

By practicing soft skills, beginning and veteran teachers alike will be more prepared for the professional aspects of teaching and will in turn educate the next generation of teachers. The end result will be more prepared teachers and better role models for students. Developing soft skills may be just one avenue to accomplish this goal, but it's certainly a great place to start!

NEXT STEPS TO INCREASING SOFT SKILLS IN THE TEACHING PROFESSION

Learning about soft skills as they apply to educators is a practice that is in line with other professions. As employers search for well-rounded workers, they are seeking individuals who have both the hard skills that make them knowledgeable about their field of expertise and the soft skills that provide a great work ethic and help them work well with others.

The soft skills in this book are often evaluated during a job interview. Being prepared to demonstrate these skills and seeking out new opportunities to practice them will assist beginning teachers in their job searches and interview preparation. If an applicant for a teaching position can model these skills in an interview situation, they are likely to portray them in the classroom as well.

Teacher-preparation institutions need to be aware of and teach these soft skills to pre-service teachers. By introducing and evaluating these skills, they will prepare well-rounded teachers for the future and will arm them with dispositions that will help them communicate, develop professional behaviors, and activate the characteristics needed to effectively teach their students. School administrators at building and district levels may train beginning teachers in soft skills and communicate the expectations of the teaching profession to those who enter their classrooms. They can share this information with mentor teachers as well, since they are an important piece of the teacher-preparation puzzle. By doing so, they will empower all teachers and impact the learning of children in classrooms. Working together, universities, schools, and others involved in preparing teachers can use these soft skills as a basis for instruction and motivation.

While the list in this book is not exhaustive, it provides a template for teachers—a jumping-off point. By being aware of how these soft skills impact the profession, we hold the keys to preparing successful teachers for a hard world today!

BIBLIOGRAPHY

American Association of Colleges for Teacher Education (AACTE) (2016). "High Quality Educator Preparation." Accessed June 14, 2018. https://www.aacte.org/resources/high-quality-educator-preparation.
Association for Teacher Educators (ATE). "Standards for Teacher Educators." Accessed June 14, 2018. https://ate1.org/resources/Documents/Standards/Teacher%20Educator%20Standards%20-%20Jan%202018.pdf.
Business Dictionary.com. Accessed July 1, 2018.
http://www.businessdictionary.com/definition/initiative.html.
Council for the Accreditation of Teacher Preparation (CAEP). http://caepnet.org/glossary?letter=D.
Dweck, Carol. (2007). *Mindset: The New Psychology of Success*. New York: Ballantine Books.
Francis, Steve. (2018). "Time Management for Teachers." Accessed July 5, 2018. http://www.timemanagementforteachers.com.au/Time_Management_For_Teachers.html.
Henriksen, Danah, and Punya Mishra. (February 2013). "Learning from Creative Teachers," *Educational Leadership*, vol. 70, number 5. Accessed June 14, 2018. http://www.ascd.org/publications/educational-leadership/feb13/vol70/num05/Learning-from-Creative-Teachers.aspx.
Howell, Kevin. (March 2017). "Is Lack of Soft Skills Hindering Millennials' Careers?" *Dice Insights*. Accessed July 3, 2018. https://insights.dice.com/2017/03/09/lack-soft-skills-hindering-millennials-careers/.
Johnson, Phillip. (1990). *Life in Classrooms*. New York: Teachers College Press.
Lamb-Sinclair, Ashley. (April 2018). "The Need for Teacher Creativity," *Education Week*. Accessed July 3, 2018. https://www.edweek.org/tm/articles/2018/04/11/the-need-for-teacher-creativity.html.
Marzano, Robert. (2010). *The Highly Engaged Classroom*. Bloomington, IN: Marzano Research.
McCloud, Carol. (2015). *Have You Filled a Bucket Today? A Guide to Daily Happiness for Kids*. Chicago: Independent Publishers Group.
Merriam-Webster Dictionary.com. Accessed July 8, 2018. https://www.merriam-webster.com/dictionary/work%20ethic.
National Communication Association (NCA). (2014). "Instructor's Corner #3: Teaching with Enthusiasm: Engaging Students, Sparking Curiosity, and Jumpstarting Motivation." Accessed July 1, 2018. https://www.natcom.org/communication-currents/instructors-corner-3-teaching-enthusiasm-engaging-students-sparking-curiosity.

National Education Association (NEA). (2012). "How Do Educators Handle Work-Related Stress?" Accessed June 14, 2018. http://neatoday.org/2012/09/07/how-do-educators-handle-work-related-stress/.

Oxford Dictionary. Accessed March 22, 2018. https://en.oxforddictionaries.com/definition/soft_skills.

Quigley, Alex. (2016). *The Confident Teacher.* New York: Routledge Publishing.

Rath, Tom, and Donald Clifton. (2004). *How Full Is Your Bucket?* New York: Gallup Press.

Roepe, Lisa Rabasca. (August 2017). *Why Soft Skills Will Help You Get the Job and the Promotion. Forbes* Magazine Online. Accessed July 1, 2018. US Army Training Manual. (1972). CONARC Soft Skills Conference. Accessed July 9, 2018. https://ipfs.io/ipfs/QmXoypizjW3WknFiJnKLwHCnL72vedxjQkDDP1mXWo6uco/wiki/Soft_skills.html.

US Department of Labor (DOL). (2012). *Skills to Pay the Bills: Mastering Soft Skills for Workplace Success.* Accessed July 3, 2018. https://www.dol.gov/odep/topics/youth/softskills/softskills.pdf.

ABOUT THE AUTHOR

Nancy Armstrong Melser began her teaching career with dolls gathered around a chalkboard. Teaching was her career choice even as a young child. Today, she works with pre-service teachers, preparing them for their future classrooms.

Nancy taught for seven years at the elementary level and co-created the gifted and talented program in her former school system. She completed her BS in elementary education at Indiana State University, and her MAE and EdD in elementary education, with minors in gifted education and educational psychology. She is currently an assistant professor at Ball State University, and has been teaching teachers for more than twenty-five years. She has a passion for working with educators in the field, and has supervised hundreds of student teachers.

Nancy has made numerous presentations at local and national conferences, and has written journal articles about effective teaching and learning. She also participates in a variety of committees at the university and community levels.

www.ingramcontent.com/pod-product-compliance
Lightning Source LLC
Chambersburg PA
CBHW032029230426

43671CB00005B/247